Published by Veda Sampson

ISBN: 0-9545846-0-0

Styling and layout by Tara Sampson
Artwork and designs by Michael Edwards (ABC Productions)
Photography by Eve Sheppard

Printed by: Templar Print and Design Ltd, Birmingham

Acknowledgements:
Deska Howe
Brian Nesbitt
Phil Creed
Bill Orgill
For all their encouragement, help and support.

This book is dedicated to my parents Miriam and Cecil Wright. You have given me so much. A big thank you for your love and inspiration in so many things.

Susannah 7/2/08

from Veda Thank you

Preface

I have always been so passionate about food and cooking, so writing this cookbook is like a dream come true for me. It not only gives me an opportunity to share a glorious part of my culture, but also provide a walk down memory lane for myself and older generations of Jamaicans. This especially includes those who have been living in England for a long time.

Having lived in England for the past forty years, I have noticed that a lot of the old Jamaican recipes are being lost. With a change in lifestyles and the larger majority of younger generations being born and brought up in England, some aspects of our culture are not being fully maintained. I am very aware of this and wanted to provide a book outlining aspects of our culture and traditions through food and cooking.

We are now living in a multi cultural society, which I feel has had a positive impact in terms of food and cooking. People are now travelling to more exotic parts of the world and sharing in lifestyles and cultures. In the past food from the Caribbean was underrated because it was unobtainable, however, thanks to specialised shops such as, Afro Caribbean, Asian, and the big supermarkets, this is no longer the case. Thus I have also aimed this book at people of different cultures who would like to try, or familiarise themselves with Jamaican cuisine.

I have provided traditional recipes with some ingredients made from scratch. However, I am aware that this will not be possible for most people. My aim in this is to provide a picture of how they were, and in some cases still are, created in Jamaica. Thus I have also provided an easier alternative or substitute, because of availability and for those who may have no, or very limited experience in this type of cooking.

My love of cooking has lead me over the years to try dishes from all over the world. I have gained a lot of pleasure in experimenting with and mixing ingredients from different countries along with those of Jamaica. Whilst the majority of the dishes are Jamaican, there are some originating from other countries which have been accepted as part of the Island's cuisine. I have also included some inventions of my own. You will also find that I have included recipes for those of you who wish to enhance dishes you are already familiar with by adding a taste of Jamaica to them.

This book is a valuable opportunity for me to look back at my roots through cooking, and bring back some aspects, which have been forgotten.

I hope it will be a valuable reference for everyone, whilst providing some insight into Jamaican culture. Most of all I hope you enjoy it!

Contents

Introduction

I was born in 1941 in St Elizabeth, Jamaica. I was the youngest of six children. Our house was situated on four acres of land in the countryside.

My father used to cultivate the land and kept a small amount of livestock such as pigs, goats, sheep, cows and chickens. He grew vegetables such as yams, sweet potato, cassava, peas, beans, escallion, herbs, peppers. As well as the family living on the produce and meat, they were also sold to provide an income.

My mother was a higgler (a street and market vendor), who took the produce and dishes she made such as fried fish and bammies to market to sell. She would in turn bring back products such as coffee, oranges, green bananas, breadfruit and other foodstuff to sell to the local people. This was done in a little makeshift shop in the yard. This would be like your modern day corner shop.

Twice weekly on a Monday and Friday my mother would go to the beach about ten miles away to buy fish and seafood caught that day by the local fishermen. This usually consisted of a variety of fish and other sea foods such as snappers, red mullet, goatfish, jack fish, parrot fish etc. lobster, crab, shrimps and prawns. She would sell them on the journey home as well as in the shop and at market.

There was also a practice in the area where local people would exchange food for payment e.g. my mother would give someone fish who had no money in exchange for vegetables we did not grow.
Another example was where my father would buy an animal and invite other people to help in its rearing and upkeep. In return they would receive a share in the meat or any offspring it might produce.

Myself and my siblings were allocated chores to help my parents. I remember from about the age of nine having to do things such as gutting, cleaning and preparing the fish for sale, scraping and sieving the cassava and picking vegetables. I delivered orders to some of the locals. I also helped my mother to sell at market late on a Friday and all day Saturday when I was not at school.

Whilst growing up in Jamaica food was important in that it provided an income for the family. It was also central to social and community events, special occasions and festivals. Whilst a lot of people did not have much money, food was plentiful. Special occasions such as weddings and christenings usually saw guests contributing food and drinks.

There are various traditions that were and still are carried out:

- We always had "Saturday Soup" which consisted of beef, mutton or corned pork. The soup contained dumplings and a large amount of vegetables such as pumpkin, yam, banana, breadfruit, sweet cassava, as well as a generous amount of fresh herbs.

- "Mannish Water" soup, which was made in very large quantities, was served at social and special occasions such as weddings, racing days etc. It was a local goat soup, which contained the head, feet and offal of the animal. There is an amusing old wives tale that the soup got its name because it provides men with great energy, strength and fertility. However, I am not aware of any surveys being carried out to back this up!

- Sundays always meant chicken, "curry goat" or beef, which were marinated and seasoned the day before. It was served with "rice and peas" and "carrot punch".

- We always had a full cooked breakfast, which kept us going until dinner in the early evening. Breakfast usually consisted of dishes such as "green banana with mackerel and fried pork", "ackee with saltfish" or "fried plantain with egg". Porridges such as oats, banana or cornmeal were also very popular.

- Important festivals such as Easter and Christmas were very exciting for me as a child. Sweet delights such as spiced bun, gizzada, coconut drops, sweet potato pudding and "blue drawers" (sweet cornmeal pudding) were in abundance. Along with the spiced bun, duck bread and coco bread ordered from the local bakery.

I was taught to cook mainly by my father from an early age. He would only use fresh products, and prepared everything from scratch. He was a very good cook who used a lot of herbs and spices to flavour and tenderise the food. Nothing was wasted when he cooked, for example peelings were fed to the pigs and chickens, bones from the meat and fish were made into soups and stock. It seemed that my father could never cook in small amounts, and was always inviting people to dinner or giving it away.

I have valued and practised these skills he passed on to me. I grow a lot of herbs such as thyme, basil and ginger for my cooking. Where possible I endeavour to prepare things from scratch e.g. I buy cassava which I scrape and grate to make my own bammies instead of buying them ready made. I always make my own seasonings, stock and pickles. Peelings from vegetables and fruit are used as compost in my garden and allotment. I have inherited my father's love of cooking, which means friends and family always arrive very hungry when they visit.

When I first came to England forty years ago, the availability of Caribbean food was very limited. I am glad to say that this is no longer the case. I want to invite people who are familiar and unfamiliar with Jamaican cuisine to share in its natural goodness, and delicious taste. For those of you who have never tried it, you will be hooked!

I have chosen most ingredients which can be found in specialised shops, markets and supermarkets. Whilst some products such as ackee, yam, and sweet potato may appear slightly expensive, they are quite filling and their nutritional value is very high.

Jamaican food, rich in nutrients, can help the body function efficiently. The variety of spicy and exotic dishes that can be created can be cooked in ways to help maintain a healthy diet:

- The food can be quite filling and rich, therefore snacking or nibbling can be reduced.

- I have outlined healthy alternative ways of cooking dishes throughout the book e.g. vegetables such as sweet potato, yam and breadfruit can be baked. Fish and seafood can be barbecued, baked or steamed. Meat can also be barbecued e.g. jerk chicken and pork.

- Marinating, seasoning, herbs and spices are an important part of Jamaican cuisine, the flavour of the food is enhanced whilst maintaining the goodness.

- Jamaican food can help boost the metabolism whilst providing necessary minerals, protein, fibre, vitamins etc.

- When used in moderation and cooked in a healthy way, its benefits are extensive in preventing and controlling certain conditions e.g. diabetes, regulating blood pressure, reducing fluid retention.

- A regular balanced diet of Jamaican food can pep up your energy levels, boost your immune system, and reduce stress.

I hope that this book will allow you to experience and bring Jamaica into your hearts and kitchen.
You will not only benefit from the taste and nutritional value, but also enjoy the whole experience from preparation to eating.

Explore it for yourself, it is an experience you will want to share.

The History Of Food In Jamaica

Jamaica is a tropical, mountainous Caribbean island steeped in history. Its cookery has been greatly influenced by settlers from all over the world (e.g. Spanish, English, American, African, Chinese French, Middle Eastern etc), who brought with them an array of colourful culinary delights which have been embraced. They also adapted recipes from their homelands to include island produced foods.

The original inhabitants of Jamaica were called Arawak Indians who dominated the island for about two thousand years before the arrival of the Europeans. Originating from the Americas the Arawaks brought with them food such as peppers, pineapples, papayas, sweet potatoes, yams, callaloo. They loved eating iguanas, turtles, fish and crabs. They grew other things such as tobacco, corn, garlic, but they mainly cultivated sweet potato and cassava. Jamaica has inherited cassava bread, known as bammies, from them. It is also thanks to the Arawaks that the well loved 'saturday soup' remains a tradition. This originated from their practice of gathering together vegetables and seasonings for various soups. They were a gentle people who lived in close communities, sharing possessions, food and often hunting and farming together.

The year 1492 saw the arrival of Christopher Columbus. The Spaniards came in search of gold, silver and spices which resulted in the indians being used as slaves. Once the Spanish established that there was not an abundance of such wealth, the Arawaks were forced to plant fruits and vegetables and work on the sugar cane plantations. Things such as the sugar cane, bananas, oranges, lemons, fig, grape and tamarind grew very successfully. The Spanish also brought livestock such as goats, pigs, cattle and horses to the island some years later.

Other European inhabitants such as the British, French and Dutch soon followed the Spaniards. Wealthy Europeans like the British and French established large plantations to meet the growing demand for sugar in Europe. This lead to the introduction of slaves from Africa between the sixteenth and eighteenth centuries.

The slaves brought with them recipes which are still a very popular part of Jamaican cuisine e.g. 'Tie-a-leaf/blue drawers' dessert, 'Turn Cornmeal' and 'Run Down'. Cooking implements and methods such as earthen ware pots used to cook food slowly known as yabba, and calabash dishes for containing and serving food were introduced by them.

The French were responsible for introducing bananas from the Canary Islands as well as some of their traditional dishes such as beef soup. The British influence is still reflected in dishes such as salt and roast meats, cakes, buns and sweet dishes.

During the eighteenth century there was a food shortage which meant things such as corn and rice had to be imported for the slaves. The export of rum and molasses provide exchanges for food such as flour and meat. New food plants such as ackee, breadfruit and mango were also introduced in the attempt to solve the problem. The slaves also grew yams and plantains.

The abolition of slavery in the mid nineteenth century meant plantation owners needed more help. This encouraged the arrival of immigrants from places such as China and India. The Chinese introduced dishes such as Shrimp and Rice, Sweet and Sour pork. There is a large amount of shops and restaurants on the island owned by them. The Indians are responsible for establishing the very popular traditional dish of 'Curried Goat' along with mango chutney and roti.

The multi-cultural nature of the Jamaican population is reflected in its rich cuisine, which is as exotic and exciting as the Island itself.

SOUPS, STARTERS AND SNACKS

MANNISH WATER

450g (1lb)	*goat meat*
1 slice	*breadfruit (can use tinned)*
1 slice	*pumpkin*
2 stalks	*escallion*
3	*green bananas*
225g (½lb)	*yellow yam*
2	*carrots*
1	*small chocho*
1	*small coco*
2	*small potatoes*
225g (½lb)	*white yam*
1	*whole hot pepper*
1	*onion*
4 pints	*water*
1 pkt	*chicken noodle soup*
2 sprigs	*fresh thyme*
1 tsp.	*annatto seeds (for colouring. If not available, grate 1 small carrot and add to meat)*
225g (½lb)	*plain flour for dumplings/spinners (see page 67)*

This soup is usually made for large numbers of people at parties or social events. To make larger amounts remember to increase quantities.

Some people in Jamaica like to add a little white rum to the soup. However, in St. Elizabeth, the rum is usually drunk on its own before the soup is served.

1. Wash meat several times. Chop it into large bite size pieces. (Alternatively you could ask the Butcher to do this for you.)
2. Bring water to boil in a very large pot. Add meat and simmer for about 2 ½ hours or until soft.
3. Take skins off bananas, peel and dice the other vegetables.
4. Skim any froth formed or bits of bone from pot.
5. Put annatto seeds into a bowl, and add ½ cup of water from the meat. Rub seeds with the back of a spoon until colour dispersed from annatto and water is an orangey /red colour. Remove and discard all the seeds and add annatto water to meat.
6. Add vegetables and salt to taste. Bring to boil, then add dumplings. Turn down heat and simmer for 1 hour.
7. Add escallions, hot peppers, thyme, chicken noodle soup and butter. Stir well and leave to simmer for 15 minutes.
8. Remove peppers and serve in cups or small bowls.

Serves 4-6.
Can be frozen and reheated.

PEPPERPOT SOUP

900g (2 lb)	callaloo or spinach
225g (½ lb)	salted pig's tail (soaked in cold water overnight)
450g (1 lb)	salt beef (can use ham hock or bacon as substitute)
1 medium	coco
½ doz.	okra (ladies fingers)
225g (½ lb)	pumpkin
225g (½ lb)	yellow yam
450g (1 lb)	breadfruit
1 small	chocho
2 large	carrots
450g (1 lb)	dasheen
1 small	onion
2 stalks	escallion
1 whole	hot pepper
1 sprig	thyme
2 cloves	garlic
3	green bananas
50g (2 oz)	coconut cream
	salt and ground pepper to taste
225g (½ lb)	plain flour for drop spoon dumplings/spinners (see page 67)

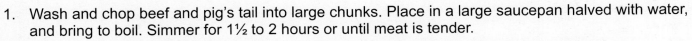

1. Wash and chop beef and pig's tail into large chunks. Place in a large saucepan halved with water, and bring to boil. Simmer for 1½ to 2 hours or until meat is tender.

2. Peel and cut vegetables into large chunks. Wash and coarsely chop calaloo or spinach.

3. Skim any froth formed on top of meat. Add callaloo or spinach and garlic, cook for 15 minutes.

4. Add vegetables and coconut cream, and simmer for 15 to 20 minutes. Stir soup about 3 times during simmering.

5. Add dumplings, whole pepper, thyme, salt and ground pepper to taste. The soup should be of medium consistency, therefore add more water if required. Stir and simmer for a further ½ hour.

Serves 8 to 10

PUMPKIN & NOODLE SOUP

1 sprig	thyme
1 clove	garlic
450g (1lb)	pumpkin – peeled and chopped
1 small	sweet potato peeled and diced
1 tbsp.	vegetable, Olive or Coconut oil
1 pkt.	soup noodles – chicken or vegetable
2	red onions peeled and chopped
1 large	tomato de-seeded and chopped
75g (3oz)	red, green and yellow peppers diced
900ml	vegetable stock
1 small tin	red kidney or butter beans
1 Stalk	escallion or spring onion
½ tsp.	freshly ground black pepper
	pinch of salt to taste
	fresh basil to garnish (optional)

1. Heat oil in large saucepan for 2-3 minutes.
2. Add pumpkin, sweet potato, onions, tomatoes, red, yellow and green peppers, escallion or spring onion. Cover and fry for a further 4-5 minutes on a low heat.
3. Add stock and noodles and bring to the boil and stir for 1-2 minutes. Lower the heat and cook for 10-15 minutes or until vegetables are soft.
4. Add thyme, black pepper, salt, and stir. Cook for a further 2-3 minutes.
5. Serve hot garnished with basil.

Serves approx. 8
Can be frozen and reheated.

Dumplings can be added if used as a main course. For a starter it can be put in a blender.

Can be served on its own, or with bread/bammies. Add cream for a richer, fuller taste if desired.

BEEF SOUP (SATURDAY SOUP)

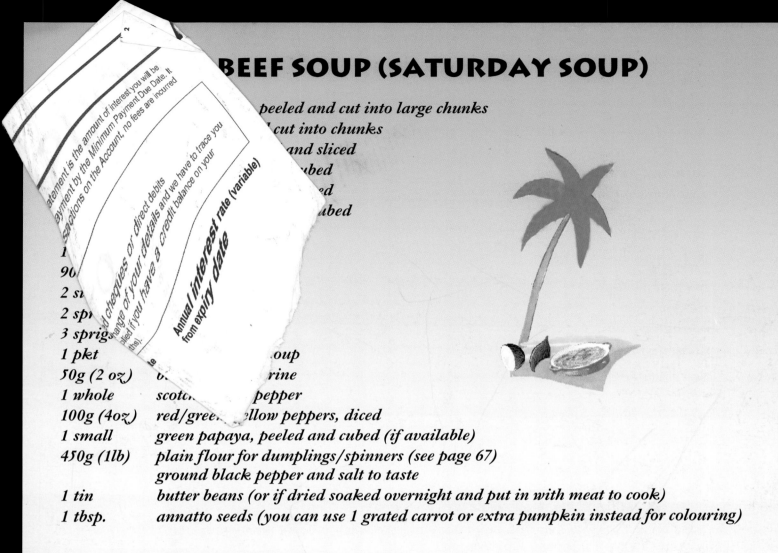

peeled and cut into large chunks
cut into chunks
and sliced
ubed
ed
ubed

1
90
2 s
2 spr
3 sprigs
1 pkt .... oup
50g (2 oz) b. .... rine
1 whole scotc....... pepper
100g (4oz) red/gree.....ellow peppers, diced
1 small green papaya, peeled and cubed (if available)
450g (1lb) plain flour for dumplings/spinners (see page 67)
ground black pepper and salt to taste
1 tin butter beans (or if dried soaked overnight and put in with meat to cook)
1 tbsp. annatto seeds (you can use 1 grated carrot or extra pumpkin instead for colouring)

1. Bring a large saucepan half filled with water to the boil. Add in meat and bones.
   Cook for 1½ to 2 hours or until meat is tender.
2. Skim any froth from top of meat.
3. Put annatto seeds in a bowl, and add ½ cup of water from meat. Rub seeds with back of a spoon until water becomes orangey/red in colour. Remove all the seeds and add annatto water to meat.
4. Add vegetables, bring to boil and simmer for ½ hour. Stir occasionally.
5. Add dumplings, scotch bonnet pepper, chicken soup noodles, butter beans (if tinned), ground pepper and salt to taste. Stir and simmer for 15 to 20 minutes until vegetables are cooked.
6. Soup should be of medium consistency, therefore add boiling water if needed.
7. Add butter/margarine, basil and thyme. Stir and simmer for 5 minutes.

*S*erves 10 - 12

PEAS SOUP

225g (½ lb)	salted pig's tail or small bacon hock. (Soaked overnight)
225g (½ lb)	red peas (kidney beans) or sam gale french beans, or gungo peas (If dried, soaked overnight)
100g (¼lb)	cornmeal for dumplings
450g (1lb)	salt beef (optional)
225g (½lb)	sweet cassava
450g (1lb)	sweet potato
450g (1 lb)	breadfruit
450g (1lb)	yam
1 small	onion
50g (2 oz)	coconut cream
1 sprig	fresh thyme
2 stalks	escallion/spring onion
1	whole hot pepper (preferably scotch bonnet pepper)
	pinch freshly ground black pepper and salt to taste
225g (½ lb)	plain flour for dumplings
	dumplings/spinners are optional (see page 67)

1. Remove water from peas and meat, and rinse with cold water.

2. Place meat and peas in a large saucepan with enough cold water to cover the ingredients. Bring to boil, then simmer for about 2 hours or until tender.

3. Peel and cut vegetables into large chunks.

4. Remove meat, cut into small pieces, and return to pot.

5. Add vegetables, stir and bring to the boil. (Add more water if required.)

6. Add dumplings, escallion, hot pepper and coconut cream. Stir well and simmer for 30 minutes.

7. Add thyme, ground black pepper and salt.

8. Remove hot pepper, stalks escallion or spring onion and serve.

Serves 6 to 8

It is not advisable to use tinned peas. Use fresh or dried.

VEGETABLE SOUP

½ tsp.	ground black or white pepper
450g (1lb)	cabbage, callaloo or spinach
1 large	onion
1 small	sweet potato
1 slice	pumpkin
2 stalks	escallion
1 small	chocho
1 large	carrot
1 small	coco
2	potatoes
225g (½lb)	yam
25g (1 oz)	coconut cream
25g (1 oz)	butter or margarine
	pinch of fresh basil
1 sprig	fresh thyme
	pinch of mixed herbs
1 pkt	powered vegetable soup
450g (1lb)	plain flour for dumplings/spinners (see page 67)

1. Wash and peel vegetables. Chop onions, escallion, cabbage, spinach or calaloo. Dice rest of vegetables.

2. Half fill a large saucepan with water and bring to boil. Lower heat.

3. Add vegetables and simmer for 20 minutes, stirring occasionally.

4. Add dumplings/spinners and simmer for 15 minutes, stirring occasionally.

5. Add vegetable soup powder, coconut cream, butter or margarine, ground pepper, mixed herbs, thyme and basil. Simmer for 5 minutes. Soup should be of medium consistency. Add more water if required. If too thin mix 1 tablespoon of flour with water and add to soup.

Serves approx. 6

Serve hot as a main meal or put in blender for a starter.
Can be served with crusty bread, bammies, pitta bread, buttered toast or croutons.

FISH SOUP/TEA

900g (2lb)	*fish including the head (can use fish of your choice)*
2 stalks	*escallion or spring onion, chopped*
1 whole	*hot pepper*
1 small	*chocho*
1 small	*turnip*
1 small	*onion*
225g (½lb)	*pumpkin*
450g (1lb)	*potato*
1	*bay leaf*
1 clove	*garlic*
1 sprig	*thyme*
3	*pimento seeds*
2 tbsp.	*lime or lemon juice*
1 pkt	*chicken noodle or vegetable soup*
	ground black pepper and salt to taste

1. Wash and soak fish in lime or lemon juice for 10 minutes. Cut fish into large pieces.

2. Half fill a large saucepan with water, and bring to boil. Add fish, garlic, pimento seeds and bay leaf. Lower heat and simmer for 30 minutes.

3. Peel and cube vegetables.

4. Strain off the stock from fish into a large dish. Remove flesh from the bones.

5. Return stock to pan and bring to boil. Add vegetables, stir and simmer for about 15 minutes, or until vegetables are tender.

6. Add flesh of fish, chicken noodle/vegetable soup, whole hot pepper, thyme, ground black pepper and salt to taste. Simmer for 5 minutes.

7. Remove hot pepper and serve.

Serves approx. 8

Serve as a main course with bammies or crusty bread.
Blend soup and add cream for a starter

CURRY PATTIES

450g (1lb)	minced meat, (of your choice e.g. goat, beef, chicken, lamb)
4 stalks	escallion or spring onion, chopped
1	red or white onion, finely chopped
2 tbsp.	vegetable/coconut oil
2	egg yolks, beaten
450g (1lb)	self-raising flour
1 sprig	thyme
2 fl.oz	milk
225g (½lb)	vegetable suet or margarine
3 cloves	garlic
2 tbsp.	curry powder
2 tsp.	turmeric powder
2 small	hot red/green chilli peppers,
100g (4 oz)	fresh bread crumbs (white or brown)

1. Heat oil in a frying pan, add meat. Fry for 10 minutes on low heat.

2. Add chopped escallion, peppers, thyme, salt, garlic and onions. Stir in curry powder and cook until meat is tender.

3. Strain off any excess oil.

4. Add bread crumbs and salt and pepper to taste. Cook for further 3 minutes. Take out and discard thyme. Leave filling to cool.

5. For pastry, mix flour, vegetable suet or margarine, turmeric and a pinch of salt. Mix well with water to form a dough. Turn onto a lightly floured surface. Roll out to approximately ¼ inch thickness. Cut round a saucer or a small side plate for required size of patties. Add some filling to half side of each disc and brush edges with water. Fold over, and then seal edges with a fork.

6. Brush the top of the patties with milk and the beaten egg yolk.

7. Bake on top shelf of the oven 400 °F/gas mark 6, for 20-25 minutes until golden brown.

*S*erve hot or cold.
Can be frozen and reheated

*F*or a vegetarian alternative replace meat with spinach or callaloo.

SALTFISH FRITTERS (STAMP AND GO)

450g (1lb)	self raising flour (or plain flour with baking powder)
2 stalks	escallions or spring onions, finely chopped
100g (4oz)	red/green/yellow peppers, diced
1 large	tomato, chopped
1 clove	garlic, crushed
2 pkts.	saltfish
1	onion, finely chopped
	pinch of salt to taste
1 tsp.	hot pepper, finely chopped
	pinch ground black pepper
½ pint	vegetable, coconut or olive oil for frying
½ tsp.	annatto, saffron or turmeric – for colouring
	Water for batter

1. Soak salt fish in water. This is usually done overnight. However, if this is not possible do so for at least 2 hours. Strain water off fish. Add clean cold water and bring to the boil. Change water after 10 minutes; repeat the process if the fish is very salty. Strain and rinse the fish, then remove skin and bones.

2. Sauté chopped peppers, garlic, onion, escallion and tomato.

3. Put flour, salt, saltfish and sautéed vegetables into a large mixing bowl. Add water and mix into a batter of medium consistency.

4. Cover the bottom of a deep frying pan or jester pot with oil. Add annatto for 1 minute and remove seeds. If you are using saffron or turmeric add them directly to batter mix.

5. Put mixture by tablespoons into the hot shallow fat and cook until golden brown on both sides. Place each one on kitchen paper to drain.

*S*erve hot or cold.

SALT FISH TARTLETS

PASTRY

225g (½lb)	*self raising flour sieved (or plain flour with 1 teaspoon baking powder)*
100g (4 oz)	*butter or margarine*
50g (2 oz)	*desiccated coconut*

FILLING

450g (1lb)	*salt fish (soaked over night in cold water)*
2 stalks	*escallion or spring onion*
	pinch freshly ground black pepper
	pinch mixed herds
	pinch of basil
1	*red onion*
½ tsp.	*turmeric*
100g (4oz)	*parmesan cheese*
100g (4oz)	*vegetable or coconut oil*
2	*fresh tomatoes, de-seeded and chopped*
100g (4oz)	*green and yellow peppers de-seeded and cubed*

1. For pastry rub butter into flour. Stir in coconut and mix in enough water to make dough.

2. Roll out pastry on a lightly floured surface and line into eight 4-inch pastry tins. Chill for 30 minutes.

3. Put into a preheated oven (375 °F/gas mark 5), and bake pastry blind for 15 minutes or until golden brown.

4. Boil fish until tender. If fish is still very salty, change water and boil again. Remove skin and bones from fish.

5. Heat oil and sauté peppers, escallion, tomatoes and onion. Add turmeric, basil and herbs.

6. Stir in fish and black pepper.

7. Add 1 tablespoon of flour and some water to the ingredients to thicken to a medium consistency.

8. Fill each case with mixture and sprinkle with parmesan cheese. Bake for 5 to 7 minutes or until golden brown on top.

Serve hot or cold.

Serve on their own, or with salad, chips or sweet potato chips.

BREADFRUIT CHIPS

1   *firm breadfruit*
vegetable or coconut oil for frying
pinch of salt

1. Peel and cut breadfruit into quarters, then remove core.
2. Cut breadfruit into thin slices and soak in salt water for ½ hour.
3. Drain and dry breadfruit.
4. Heat oil, then put in breadfruit.
5. Fry until chips are golden brown. Remove and drain.

COCONUT CHIPS

1. Remove white flesh of coconut from the brown shell.
2. Cut coconut into thin slices/strips.
3. Wash and leave to drain.
4. Fry lightly in hot oil until chips are crisp.
5. Remove, and sprinkle lightly with salt.

*S*erve hot or cold.

1   *dry coconut*
vegetable or coconut oil for frying
pinch of salt

PLANTAIN CHIPS

1   *green plantain*
vegetable or coconut oil for frying
pinch of salt

1. Remove skin from plantain and cut into very thin slices.
2. Wash and soak in salt water for ½ hour.
3. Drain and dry plantain.
4. Fry in hot oil until golden brown.
   Serve hot or cold as starter or snack.

*T*o cut down on oil, sprinkle coconut chips with salt and bake in oven (350 °F/ gas mark 4) for 20 minutes or until slightly brown.

CARIBBEAN PARCELS

1 tbsp.	coconut milk (alternatively use tinned or coconut powder. Or add boiling water to coconut cream)
2 stalks	escallion or spring onion chopped
1	meat or vegetable stock cube
2	carrots grated
100g (4oz)	plain flour
1 large	egg
½ tsp.	turmeric
5 fl oz (¼ pint)	milk
1	potato, grated
1	onion chopped
1 small	tomato diced
10fl oz (½ pint)	vegetable or coconut oil
1 small	egg for brushing parcels
2 tsp.	cornflour or flour to thicken
100g (4 oz)	red/green/yellow peppers diced
1 small	scotch bonnet pepper de-seeded and chopped finely.
225g (½ lb)	lean minced meat of your choice (e.g. goat, chicken, pork, beef or lamb)

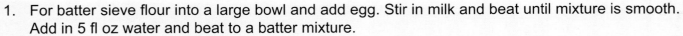

1. For batter sieve flour into a large bowl and add egg. Stir in milk and beat until mixture is smooth. Add in 5 fl oz water and beat to a batter mixture.

2. Heat 3 tablespoons oil in frying pan. Add minced meat, vegetables, turmeric and pepper. Cook for 5 minutes, stirring occasionally.

3. Mix stock cube in a cup of boiling water. Blend in 2 teaspoons of cornflour or flour with 4 tablespoons of the stock. Add rest of the stock to the pan and bring to boil.

4. Add cornflour/ flour mixture to pan and cook for 2 minutes stirring all the time.

5. Simmer for 10 minutes then leave to cool.

6. Heat a little oil in a frying pan and drain off excess. Pour in a little batter mix and spread thin evenly over base. Cook underside until golden brown. Take out of frying pan - do not cook the other side. Continue process until all batter is used.

7. Put each pancake cooked side up on a surface and spread equal amounts of filling down middle of each. Fold side edges of pancake over filling, and then fold over bottom and top edges, making sure the entire filling is covered.

8. Brush each parcel with beaten egg and chill for 1 hour. Heat oil in deep pan or fryer. Fry each parcel in hot oil for 2-3 minutes or until golden brown. Drain on kitchen paper.

PINEAPPLE AND CHILLI PEPPER PIZZA

TOPPING

2	chillies, one red and one green, deseeded and chopped
1	clove garlic crushed or ¼ teaspoon garlic powder
4	pineapple rings, cut into pieces
1	onion quartered and sliced
2	fresh tomatoes, chopped
3 stalks	escallion/spring onion chopped
6 tbsp.	tomato puree (paste)
100g (4oz)	mozzarella cheese
100g (4 oz)	cheddar cheese
75g (3oz)	sweet corn
¼ tsp.	dried oregano
1 tbs.	olive or vegetable oil
2 sprigs	basil chopped finely
	pinch ground black pepper
	pinch salt to taste
75g (3 oz)	red/green/yellow peppers diced

DOUGH

225 g (½ lb)	plain flour
1 tsp.	yeast
¼ tsp.	salt
2 tsp.	olive oil
1 tsp.	sugar
150ml (5 fl oz)	hand hot water

1. For dough put yeast and sugar in warm water and cover for 5 minutes.

2. Sift flour in a large bowl, add salt and rub in oil. Add water and yeast mixture and mix to form dough.

3. Knead dough lightly, and then roll out to fit 10-inch tray or ovenproof plate. Cover with cling film or warm damp tea towel.

4. For topping heat oil in a frying pan or saucepan. Sauté onion, escallion/spring onion, tomato, red, green, yellow peppers, garlic and corn, for 5 minutes. Add dried oregano.

5. Blind bake dough in oven for 5 minutes.

6. Brush surface of dough with a little olive oil, and cover with tomato puree.

7. Spread sautéed vegetables over dough. Scatter with grated cheese. Add chillies and pineapple all over, then sprinkle over chopped basil.

8. Bake on top shelf of oven for 15 minutes or until cheese is melted and golden brown.

Serve hot or cold. Cut into wedges.

Can be eaten on its own or with salad, sweet potato wedges or chips.

SOLOMON GUNDY

1	hot pepper, deseeded and finely chopped
1 tbsp.	pimento seeds or cloves
50g (2 oz)	onion, finely chopped
450g (1lb)	red herring
1 tbsp.	oil
2 fl.oz	vinegar
1 tbsp.	rum (optional)
½ tsp.	freshly ground black pepper
50g (2 oz)	sweet peppers (red/yellow/green), chopped

1. Wrap herring in newspaper. Light one end of the newspaper.
2. When the newspaper is totally burned, peel off the skin of the herring, remove bones and flake flesh.
3. Put vinegar, onion, sweet pepper and pimento seeds/cloves in a saucepan and bring to the boil. Simmer for 2 minutes.
4. Mix all ingredients together. Cover and leave overnight.
5. Blend or grind the ingredients to a smooth paste.
6. Spoon into a jar and store in the fridge.

Serve spread on crackers or toast. (See page 81 for water crackers)

Solomon Gundy can also be used as a dip, and to add flavour to fish and seafood dishes.

Roasting the herring in newspaper is the traditional method. However, you can bake it in foil in the oven or scald it in boiling water, to remove bones and skin.

FRIED SARDINES OR SPRATS WITH CRACKERS

4 large	sardines or 900g (2 lb) sprats
1 large	onion, chopped
3 stalks	escallion or spring onion, chopped
2	green chillies, whole
1	cotch bonnet pepper, deseeded and chopped
100g (4oz)	sweet pepper (red/yellow/green)
2 tbsp.	flour
2 tsp.	salt
¼ tsp	ground black pepper
6	pimento seeds (optional)
1	lemon or lime juiced
	lemon or lime slices to garnish
	coconut or vegetable oil for frying

*S*erves 4

1. Scrape and clean sardines (you can ask the fishmonger to do this for you).
2. Sprinkle salt and black pepper over fish.
3. Put flour on a large plate. Coat fish with flour, shaking off any excess.
4. Heat oil in a frying pan.
5. Fry fish for about 10 minutes or until crisp, turning them over during frying.
6. Remove fish and drain on kitchen paper.
7. Fry onions, escallion/spring onion, peppers and pimento.
8. Put fish on a serving plate and spread over fried vegetables. Sprinkle over lemon or lime juice. Garnish with lemon or lime slices.
9. Serve hot or cold with water crackers. (See page 81)

SARDINE PATE

1 (225g/8oz)	tin sardines in oil
50g (2oz)	butter
½	lemon, juiced
	pinch of grated nutmeg
	salt to taste
	ground black pepper to taste
	bay leaves to garnish (optional)

1. Blend all the ingredients together until smooth.
2. Put into a small dish and garnish with bay leaves.
3. Put into fridge to chill before serving.
4. Serve with toast or water crackers (See page 81)

THREE BEANS SALAD

225g (½ lb)	dry kidney beans. Soak in cold water overnight.
3 tbsp.	coconut powder or 75g (3oz) of coconut cream
	pinch parsley for garnish (optional)
1 large	red onion sliced
225g (½lb)	black eye peas
	pinch of salt
1	green pepper sliced
1 tbsp.	lime and lemon juice
½ tsp.	freshly ground black pepper
225 (½lb)	butter beans soaked in cold water overnight

1. Wash kidney, butter beans and black eye peas. Place in a saucepan of cold water, add pinch of salt and coconut powder/cream, cover and boil until tender. Remove from heat and drain off water.

2. Put beans in a large dish and mix with red onion, and green pepper. Sprinkle with lime and lemon juice then add freshly ground black pepper to taste. Garnish with parsley.

Serve warm or chilled.

Can be served with salad, meat, fish or vegetarian dishes.

TANGY AVOCADO SALAD

2 sprigs	fresh mint chopped finely
½	iceberg lettuce
2	ripe avocado
3	oranges
4	grapefruit
½ tsp.	sugar
½	lime
½	lemon
3 tsp.	vegetable oil
	salt to taste
	pinch of ground black pepper

1. Tear or chop lettuce and put in a salad bowl.
2. Remove skins and stone from avocados. Cut flesh into slices or dice.
3. Remove peel and pith from oranges and grapefruit, holding them over avocado so juice falls over (to prevent avocado discolouring). Remove orange and grapefruit segments and cut into halves.
4. Add avocado, orange and grapefruit to lettuce.
5. Mix vegetable oil with juice of lime and lemon, sugar, fresh mint and ground black pepper. Add salt to taste. Then spoon over salad.

Serves 6

Serve as a starter or as side salad.

STUFFED PEPPERS

4 medium	red or green peppers
100g (4 oz)	bread crumbs or boiled rice
2	onions finely chopped
3 stalks	escallions finely chopped
2	tomatoes finely chopped
1 clove	garlic
½ tsp	turmeric
50ml (12floz)	vegetable or coconut oil
2	green chillies de-seeded and finely chopped
½ oz	fresh root ginger grated or
½ tsp	ginger powder
	salt to taste

**STUFFED PEPPERS &
STUFFED PAW PAW**

1. Heat half amount of oil in a frying pan. Add whole peppers and fry for about 5 minutes or until brown on all sides.
2. Remove peppers and drain on kitchen paper.
3. Add rest of oil to pan. Add chillies, garlic, onion, tomato, escallion, and fry until tender. Stir in ginger and turmeric.
4. Add breadcrumbs or boiled rice to pan with 4 fl oz water and stir well. Add salt to taste. Cook for 5 minutes or until liquid absorbed.
5. Cut tops off peppers and remove seeds.
6. Stuff peppers with filling and replace tops.
7. Stand peppers on slightly greased baking tray or ovenproof dish. Bake in preheated oven (350ºF/gas mark 4 for 15 to 20 minutes or until soft.

Serves 4

Serve as starter or light meal.

STUFFED PAW PAW (PAPAYA)

2	*unripe paw paw (papaya)*
75g (3oz)	*boiled rice*
225g (8 oz)	*lean minced meat of your choice (beef, pork, chicken, lamb or vegetarian mince)*
1	*onion, chopped*
1	*clove garlic, chopped*
2	*tomatoes, chopped*
2	*vegetable stock cubes*
2 tbsp.	*coconut or vegetable oil*
1	*hot red or green pepper, deseeded and chopped*
½	*sweet pepper, deseeded and diced (red/green/yellow)*
2 tsp.	*chives, snipped*
	ground black pepper and salt to taste

1. Remove seeds from paw paw, cut in half lengthways. Parboil in salted water for 5 minutes. Dry and place in a greased baking tray or oven proof dish.

2. Heat oil in a frying pan. Add meat and fry for 5 minutes until browned. Add vegetables, chives, vegetable stock cubes and 2 fl oz of boiling water. Simmer for 5 minutes.

3. Stir in boiled rice. Add salt and black pepper to taste.

4. Spoon the meat filling into paw paw halves.

5. Bake in preheated oven (350 °F/ gas mark 4) for 20 to 25 minutes.

Serves 4

Serve hot

VEGETABLE AND FRUIT KEBABS

2 small	onions cut into quarters
1 small	red pepper deseeded and cut into large pieces
1 small	green pepper deseeded and cut into large pieces
2	ripe firm plantains, peeled and cut into large chunks
½ small	ripe pineapple, peeled, cored and cut into cubes or small tin of pineapple cubes, drained.
1	sweet corn sliced into 1-inch pieces
1 small	sweet potato cut into large chunks
6 tbsp.	oil
½	lemon
½	lime
2 tbsp.	orange juice
1 sprig	fresh basil
1 sprig	fresh rosemary
	ground black pepper
	salt to taste

1. Blanch sweet potato, onion, sweet corn and peppers in boiling water for 3 minutes. Drain and dry on kitchen paper.
2. Thread all ingredients on kebab skewers.
3. Mix oil, orange juice, lemon and lime juice, black pepper and salt. Add basil and rosemary and stir. Leave covered for 20 minutes.
4. Place kebabs in a shallow dish and spoon over marinade. Cover and leave for at least 1 hour
5. Grill or barbecue for 8 to 10 minutes, or until evenly browned. Turn kebabs and brush with marinade during cooking.

Serve hot

Serve as a starter or side dish.

SWEET POTATO WEDGES

900g (2lb)	sweet potatoes
100g (4 oz)	plain flour
	pinch of dried herbs
1	vegetable stock cube
	pinch of salt
	pinch of black pepper
½ pint	vegetable or coconut oil

1. Wash and boil potatoes in skins for 7 minutes.
2. Drain and leave to cool. Then cut into wedges.
3. Mix flour, herbs, vegetable stock cube and pinch of salt in a plastic food/ freezer bag.
4. Heat oil in chip pan or deep saucepan.
5. Put potato wedges in bag with mixture, and shake until wedges are covered.
6. Put into hot oil and fry until crisp and golden brown.
7. Remove and drain on kitchen paper.

*T**ip***

*C**ut down on fat by placing potato wedges on a lightly greased baking tray and bake in oven for 20 minutes (turning over half way through) on 400° F/gas mark 6.*

PEPPER & ESCALLION TWISTS

3 stalks	escallion or spring onions
1	sweet red pepper
100g (4oz)	plain flour
50g (2oz)	butter
3	egg yolks
1	egg white
	pinch chilli powder
	pinch mixed herbs
50g (2oz)	cheddar cheese, grated

1. Grill red pepper whole until the skin wrinkles all over. Leave to cool.
2. Sift flour and salt into a bowl. Mix in mixed herbs and grated cheese.
3. Rub in butter until mixture resembles breadcrumbs. Add egg yolks, chilli powder and enough water to form a dough.
4. Roll out on a lightly floured surface into a rectangular shape approx. 12 x 10-inch. Cut in half lengthways. Cut each half into thin strips.
5. Remove skin from pepper and cut flesh into thin strips.
6. Cut escallion or spring onions into thin strips.
7. Twist together pastry strips with pepper and escallion/spring onion strips.
8. Brush with beaten egg white.
9. Place on greased baking sheets.
10. Bake in a preheated oven 400°F/ gas mark 6) for 10 to 15 minutes until golden brown.
11. Remove and put on wire rack to cool.

*M**akes 60 to 70. Serve on their own or with dips.*

MEAT DISHES

CURRIED GOAT ✓

2 stalks	escallion or spring onion, chopped
1	hot pepper, finely chopped
1 medium	onion, chopped
2 cloves	garlic, chopped
2 ½ tbsp.	curry powder
900g (2lb)	goat meat
1 sprig	thyme
3 tbsp.	oil
1 ½ tsp.	salt
2 tbsp.	lime juice
1 small	chocho, diced (optional)
1 large	tomato, chopped
½ tsp.	ground black pepper

1. Wash and cut goat meat into cubes.
2. Season the meat with onion, escallion/spring onion, hot pepper, garlic, curry powder. Add lime juice and stir well. Leave to marinate for at least 2 hours (even more beneficial if done overnight).
3. Heat oil in jester pot or heavy saucepan.
4. Remove meat from seasoning and brown in the hot oil.
5. Cover the meat with boiling water and simmer for 2 hours or until meat is tender.
6. Add seasoning and chocho to the meat and stir. Add thyme, tomato, margarine or butter, black pepper and salt. Simmer for a further ½ hour.
7. Add more water if required. The curried goat should be reduced to a stew-like medium consistency.
8. Remove thyme and serve hot.

Serves 4

Goes well with boiled white rice, bammies, roti, boiled green bananas/sweet potato/yam, and roast breadfruit.

CHICKEN WITH RICE & PEAS

1 large	chicken (3 ½ to 4lb) cut into approx. 12 portions
2 stalks	escallion or spring onions, chopped
1 large	onion, chopped
1	hot pepper, finely chopped
100g (4oz)	sweet pepper (red/yellow/green), chopped
2 cloves	garlic, chopped
½ inch	root ginger or ½ teaspoon ginger powder
1	fresh tomato
1 small	tin tomatoes, chopped
100g (4oz)	flour
1 tbsp.	annatto seeds or ½ tablespoon turmeric to colour
½ pint	vegetable or coconut oil
½ tsp.	ground black pepper
1 tbsp.	salt

For rice and peas recipe see page 64

1. Wash chicken and drain.
2. Put onion, escallion/spring onion, hot pepper, ginger, garlic, sweet pepper, salt, black pepper into large bowl. If using turmeric add to seasoning at this point. Add chicken and mix well. Leave to marinate for at least 2 hours (preferably overnight).
3. Heat oil in jester pot or large heavy frying pan.
4. Put flour on large plate. Remove chicken from marinated seasoning, and lightly coat in the flour. Shake off any excess flour.
5. If using annatto seeds, place them in the hot oil for 1 minute. Remove all seeds.
6. Fry chicken pieces in the oil until golden brown on each side. Remove and place on plate or dish.
7. Lower heat, add marinated seasoning, fresh and tinned tomato. Add ¾ pint boiling water and simmer for 5 minutes.
8. Add chicken pieces and thyme, stirring occasionally, simmer on low heat for 15 minutes or until chicken is tender.
9. Remove thyme and serve hot with the rice and peas.

*S*erves 6

*C*an be frozen and reheated.

CHICKEN AND YAM CASSEROLE

6	portions skinless chicken
675 g (1½ lb)	yam, diced
100g (4 oz)	pumpkin, diced
2 tbsp.	coconut or vegetable oil
1 large	onion, thinly sliced
2 cloves	garlic, chopped
3	pimento seeds/ cloves
4 stalks	escallion or spring onions, chopped
1 small	chocho, diced
1	whole green chilli pepper, finely chopped
1 sprig	thyme
2 sprigs	basil finely chopped
½ tsp.	freshly ground black pepper
1 small	tin of butter beans
1 tsp.	dry jerk seasoning (see page 110)
¼ tsp.	salt
1 pint	chicken stock

1. Wash chicken and sprinkle with jerk seasoning.
2. Heat oil in a large frying pan.
3. Fry chicken portions for 10 minutes or until browned on all sides. Remove and place in an ovenproof casserole dish.
4. Fry onion, garlic, 3 stalks escallion/spring onion, chilli pepper and cho cho for 3 to 4 minutes, or until soft. Remove and put into casserole dish with chicken.
5. Add yam slices and pumpkin to frying pan. Cook for 3 minutes on each side or until evenly browned. Put into casserole dish.
6. Add thyme, pimento seeds /cloves, 1 sprig basil, black pepper, salt and butter beans to dish. Pour over chicken stock.
7. Cook in oven for 30 to 40 minutes (400ºF/gas mark 6), or until meat and vegetables are tender.
8. Sprinkle over remaining chopped basil and escallion/spring onion to garnish.

Serves 6

Serve hot

Can also be served with crusty bread or white rice.

JERK CHICKEN

3	whole chickens or portions of breast, leg and thigh
1	lemon
1	lime
225g (½ lb)	wet jerk seasoning (See page 110)
	(Can use dried)

1. If using whole chickens, cut into portions.

2. Slice lemon and lime and put into large bowl of water. Add chicken portions and wash thoroughly. Drain portions and dry with kitchen paper.

3. Spoon and spread jerk seasoning over both sides of each chicken portion. Leave to marinate for at least 2 hours (preferably overnight in the fridge).

4. Place chicken portions on a grill over burning coals/barbecue, to obtain a smoky flavour. Or bake on a grid in the oven 400°F/Gas mark 6

5. Turn each portion of chicken frequently to prevent burning.

6. When crisp and cooked through put portions aside on grill or cover with foil in the oven on low heat, to keep them hot.

Serves approx. 12 to 14

Serve with salad, hard dough bread, coco bread or white rice Delicious with mango chutney (page 114), pickled pepper (page 113), pineapple salsa (page 116) or dips (page 115).

FRIED CHICKEN

1.75kg (4 lb)	*chicken or portions*
1	*lemon*
1	*lime*
100g (4 oz)	*dried jerk seasoning (See page 110)*
1 pint	*coconut or vegetable oil*
175g (6oz)	*flour*

1. Cut chicken into small pieces.
2. Cut lemon and lime and put to a large bowl of water. Add chicken and wash thoroughly. Drain and dry with kitchen paper.
3. Mix flour and dried jerk seasoning together. Coat each piece of chicken with mixture.
4. Heat oil until very hot.
4. Fry pieces for 10 to 12 minutes, or until cooked through and golden brown.
5. Place pieces on kitchen paper to drain.

JERK & FRIED CHICKEN

CHICKEN GUMBO

1.75 kg (4 lb)	chicken cut into pieces
225g (8 oz)	okra, trimmed and chopped
2	onions, chopped
3 stalks	escallion or spring onion chopped
2	red peppers diced
2 cloves	garlic, crushed
2	chilli peppers, deseeded and chopped
3 sticks	celery, chopped
2 tsp.	paprika pepper
½ tsp.	tabasco sauce
2 tsp.	ground black pepper
2 tbsp	flour
6 tbsp.	coconut or vegetable oil
4 pints	chicken stock
2 sprigs	fresh parsley chopped
225g (8 oz)	cooked long grain rice

1   Wash and dry chicken.

2. Mix salt, paprika and ground black pepper together. Sprinkle over chicken pieces.

3. Heat 4 tablespoons of oil in frying pan. Add chicken pieces and fry until evenly browned on both sides.

4. Put remaining oil in pan. Add half amount of onions, celery, okra, chillies, red pepper, and sauté for 5 minutes or until soft.

5. Sprinkle flour into sautéed vegetables, and cook until mixture is golden brown.

6. Put chicken stock and remaining vegetables into a large saucepan and bring to boil.

7. Add chicken pieces and simmer for 1 hour.

8. Add sautéed vegetables and flour mixture. Simmer for 15 minutes.

9. Add rice, escallion/spring onions and Tabasco sauce. Cook for a further 15 minutes.

10. Sprinkle with fresh parsley.

Serve with salad, bread rolls or crusty bread.
Delicious with mango chutney (page 114), pickled pepper (page 113)

Serves 6
Serve with crusty bread.

PORK CHOPS WITH BUTTER BEANS

6	thick loin pork chops with rind
225g (½ lb)	dried butter beans, soaked in cold water overnight. Or 1 large tin of butter beans.
1 large	fresh tomato, chopped
2 cloves	garlic, crushed
100g (4 oz)	sweet peppers green/yellow/red
1 tsp.	fresh root ginger or ginger powder
1 sprig	fresh rosemary, chopped coarsely
1 sprig	fresh thyme, chopped coarsely
1 tbsp.	lime juice
25g (1 oz)	coconut cream
50g (2oz)	flour
1 tsp.	salt
½ tsp.	turmeric
½ tsp.	ground black pepper
4 tbsp.	coconut or vegetable oil
	sprigs fresh rosemary to garnish (optional)

1. If using dried butter beans rinse them in fresh cold water after soaking. Place in saucepan and cover with water. Bring to the boil then add coconut cream and pinch of salt. Simmer until beans are tender. Remove them from water.
2. Wash pork chops, and dry on kitchen paper.
3. Mix together flour, black pepper, mixed herbs, salt and turmeric on a large plate or dish. Coat each pork chop with mixture.
4. Heat oil in large frying pan or jester pot.
5. Fry chops on each side until golden brown.
6. Remove chops and place in an oven proof casserole dish with lid.
7. Sauté onions, escallions, tomato, sweet pepper, garlic, ginger in remaining oil.
8. Spread butter beans and sautéed vegetables over pork chops.
9. Remove any excess oil from frying pan/jester pot. Add ½ pint water and bring to the boil, then pour over pork chops. Add thyme and rosemary. Cover and put in oven, 375 °F/gas mark 5, for 45 minutes or until meat is tender.
10. Serve hot. Spoon sauce over chops and garnish with fresh rosemary.

As an option use button mushrooms instead of butter beans.

JERK PORK

2.3kg (5lb)	shoulder or leg of Pork
1	lemon
1	lime
6 tbsp.	wet or dry jerk seasoning (See page 110)
1 tbsp.	salt

1. Cut lemon and lime and place in a large bowl of water. Add pork and wash thoroughly.

2. Dry pork, then rub salt all over.

3. Rub jerk seasoning over pork. Leave to marinate for at least 2 hours (preferably over night).

4. Cook on grid over hot coals/barbecue. Or place on baking tray in preheated oven 425°F/ gas mark 7 for 15 to 20 minutes to form crisp skin. Turn temperature down to 350°F/gas mark 4, for 1 ½ hours or until cooked through.

5. Chop into small pieces.

Serves 6 to 8

Goes well with, salads, rice, vegetables, chips/potato wedges.
Try it with Jamaican pickled pepper to add extra kick - (page 113)

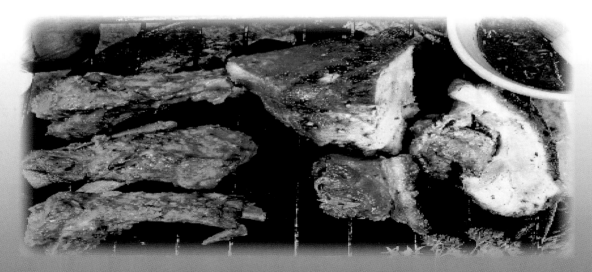

JERK PORK & SPARE RIBS

SPARE RIBS ✓

1.75 kg (4 lb)	pork spare ribs
1	lime or lemon
1 tsp	turmeric
3 tbsp.	wet or dry jerk seasoning (see page 110)
5 tbsp.	oil
	sweet and tangy marinade (page 111) (optional) or
	guava sauce (page 112) (optional)

1. Wash spare ribs and sprinkle with lime juice.

2. Put spare ribs in a large bowl. Rub jerk seasoning all over spare ribs. Sprinkle over turmeric and stir. Leave to marinade for at least 2 hours or preferably overnight.

3. Fry spare ribs in oil until evenly brown.

4. Brush with a sauce or marinade (optional).

5. Arrange in roasting tin, cover with foil and cook in oven for 30 minutes (350°F/gas mark 4). Or wrap in foil and cook on barbecue for 10 to 15 minutes.

6. Serve hot with barbecue sauce (page 111) or sauce of your choice.

*S*erves 5 to 6

STEW PEAS

450g (1 lb)	red kidney beans or sam gale french beans. If dried soak over night in cold water.
4	salted pig's tails, chopped (soaked overnight)
225g (½ lb)	salt Beef (optional) (soaked overnight)
1	onion, chopped
2 stalks	escallion, chopped
1	whole hot pepper e.g. scotch bonnet or chilli
1 sprig	thyme
1 sprig	marjoram or oregano (can use dried)
50g (2 oz)	coconut cream pinch black pepper
225g (½ lb)	flour for dumplings/spinners (see page 67)

1. Place meat and beans in a large saucepan, cover with fresh water and bring to the boil.

2. Skim any froth formed in pan. Add coconut cream, simmer for 2 hours or until meat and beans are soft.

3. Add dumplings/spinners, onion, escallion, thyme, marjoram/oregano, black pepper and whole hot pepper. Simmer for 15 to 20 minutes until liquid is reduced to a stew consistency. Remove whole hot pepper and thyme. Stir well.

Serves 4

Traditionally served on a bed of white rice.
Can also be served with boiled green bananas or sweet potato

Can be frozen and reheated.

BELLY DRAFT OF PORK WITH MACKEREL OR SALT FISH

4 slices	belly draft of pork (each slice cut into 3 pieces)
1 whole	salt mackerel or 450g (1lb) of salt fish (soaked overnight in cold water)
1 dozen	okra (Ladies fingers)
2 stalks	escallion, chopped
100g (4oz)	sweet pepper, red/yellow/green
1 large	onion, chopped
1	scotch bonnet pepper, deseeded and chopped
1 clove	garlic
2	fresh tomatoes, diced
5 tbsp	oil
	pinch mixed herbs
	pinch black pepper
	salt to taste.

1. Boil mackerel or salt fish in fresh water for 5 minutes. Change water; add okra with the fish and return to boil for a further 5 minutes. Remove pan from heat and change water again, then leave to cool.

2. Heat oil in frying pan or jester pot. Fry pieces of belly draft for 10 minutes or until crisp and golden brown on each side. Remove and set aside.

3. Remove skin and bones from fish, and then flake the flesh.

4. Sauté onion, escallion, garlic, tomato, sweet pepper, scotch bonnet pepper. Add mixed herbs, black pepper and salt to taste.

5. Add flaked fish, okra and belly draft pieces to sautéed vegetables and stir. Cook for 2 to 3 minutes until warmed through.

Serves 4

Serve hot with rice, bammies, boiled vegetables or roasted breadfruit.

Can be frozen and reheated.

CARIBBEAN ROAST PORK

1.5 kg (3lb)	pork joint
2 cloves	garlic crushed
2 stalks	escallion or spring onions chopped
1	onion, sliced
5 fl oz	pineapple juice
2 tbsp	honey
5	pimento seeds or cloves
1 tsp.	fresh root ginger grated or ginger powder
1 tsp.	cinnamon
1 tsp.	turmeric
1 tbsp.	tamarind sauce or soy sauce
2 tbsp	oil
1	lemon
1	lime

1. Put ½ lemon and lime in a large bowl of water. Wash pork thoroughly.

2. Heat pineapple juice, honey, tamarind sauce/soy sauce, and cinnamon in a saucepan. Stir in pimento seeds/cloves and bring to boil. Leave to cool.

3. Stir in ginger, garlic, escallion, onion and juice of remaining lemon and lime.

4. Place pork into a large dish/container, cover with the marinade. Cover and place in fridge for at least 4 hours, turning frequently and covering pork with the marinade. Ideally it would be better marinated over night.

5. Remove pork from marinade.

6. Heat oil in a roasting tin in oven.

7. Add pork and roast for 1 ½ to 2 hours, or until cooked through. (375 °F/gas mark 5).

8. Raise oven temperature to 400 °F/gas mark 6, fifteen to twenty minutes before cooking completed, until pork browned on top.

Serve hot or cold

Serve with vegetables or salad. Goes well with a variety of chutney, dips or salsa - see pages 114-116.

PORK WITH GINGER

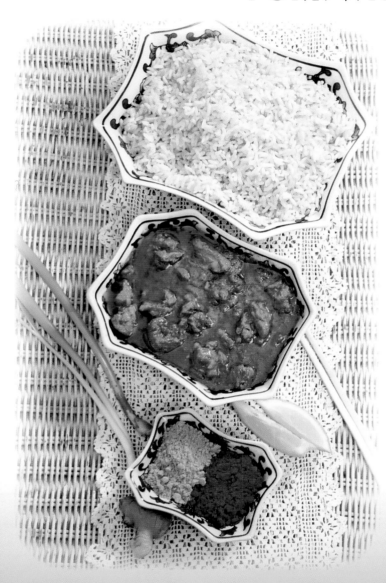

450g (2lb)	diced pork
50g (2oz)	root ginger, grated
	or 1 teaspoon of ginger powder
1 tsp.	turmeric
3 stalks	escallion or spring onion, chopped
1 small	cho cho, diced
1 large	onion, chopped
1	chilli pepper, deseeded and chopped
2 cloves	garlic
4	pimento seeds or cloves
1 tsp.	soy sauce
½ tsp.	salt
6 tbsp.	coconut or vegetable oil
3 sprigs	thyme
1 sprig	rosemary

1. Put diced pork into a large dish or container with lid.

2. Mix ginger, soy sauce, turmeric, escallion, chilli, onion, garlic, cho cho, salt and pimento seeds/cloves. Add to diced pork and stir well. Leave to marinate for at least 2 hours, preferably over night.

3. Heat oil in a deep frying pan or jester pot.

4. Remove diced pork from marinade and fry for 5 to 7 minutes or until golden brown.

5. Add marinated vegetables and ½ cup of boiling water. Add thyme and rosemary. Simmer for 20 to 25 minutes or until pork is tender.

6. Remove thyme and rosemary.

Goes well with white rice, boiled green banana or boiled sweet cassava.

Serve hot
Serves 4

LAMB CHOPS WITH SAFFRON/TURMERIC RICE

8	lamb cutlets
1	onion, chopped
75g (3oz)	sweet pepper, diced
1 tsp.	root or powdered ginger
2 cloves	garlic, crushed
1 tsp.	ground black pepper
1 sprig	rosemary
3 tbsp	flour
4 tbsp	oil
	salt to taste
450g (1lb)	white long grain rice
3	lamb or vegetable stock cubes
	watercress or parsley to garnish (optional)
3 stalks	escallion or spring onion, chopped
	pinch saffron or 1 teaspoon turmeric

1. Mix peppers, onion, garlic, escallion, ginger, black pepper and salt. Add lamb cutlets and stir well. Leave to marinate for at least 2 hours.

2. Put flour in food/freezer bag. Remove cutlets from marinade and place in bag with flour. Shake bag well to coat cutlets.

3. Heat oil in large frying pan. Add cutlets and fry until browned on both sides. Remove and set aside.

4. Sauté marinated vegetables. Return cutlets to frying pan with vegetables.

5. Dissolve 2 stock cubes in ½ pint boiling water and pour over cutlets. Cover and simmer for 15 to 20 minutes or until cutlets are tender and stock is reduced to a medium consistency gravy.

6. Put rice in medium size saucepan, cover with water. Add 1 stock cube, salt, saffron or turmeric. Stir and bring to the boil. Cook on low heat for 30 minutes or until rice is tender and liquid absorbed.

7. Serve cutlets and rice hot, garnished with watercress or parsley.

*S*erves 4

PEPPERED STEAK

900g (2lb)	frying or sirloin steaks
1 tbsp.	crushed pepper corns
½ tbsp.	root or powdered ginger
100g (4oz)	sweet peppers cut into strips (red/green/yellow)
3 cloves	garlic, crushed
2 stalks	escallion or spring onion, chopped
1	onion, sliced
3 tbsp.	flour
3 tbsp.	coconut or vegetable oil
1 sprig	thyme
1 sprig	marjoram (or ½ tsp. dried)
1	lime or lemon
	pinch saffron or turmeric
	pinch salt

1. Put steaks in a large bowl or container with lid.
2. Mix peppercorns, garlic, escallion, ginger, salt, saffron or turmeric. Sprinkle over lime or lemon juice and stir well. Spread mixture over both sides of steaks, and leave to marinade in fridge for at least 2 hours or overnight.
3. Put flour on large plate. Coat each steak lightly and knock off any excess flour.
4. Heat oil in large frying pan or jester pot. Fry steaks on both sides until browned. Remove from oil
5. Add pepper strips and onion to frying pan and sauté for 3 minutes.
6. Return steak to frying pan and cover with sautéed peppers and onion. Add thyme, marjoram and ½ pint boiling water. Simmer for 15 to 20 minutes or until meat is tender and liquid absorbed.

Serves 4

Serve hot with boiled rice, or sweet potato wedges, roast or boiled vegetables. Can be frozen and reheated.

COW FOOT

1.5 kg (3lb)	cow foot, scraped and chopped into large chunks. (you can ask the butcher to do this for you)
1	onion, chopped
1 stalk	escallion, chopped
1	scotch bonnet pepper, deseeded and chopped
1 large	tomato, chopped
1	cho cho, diced
2 cloves	garlic, crushed
1 large	potato, diced
½ tsp.	ground black pepper
½ tsp.	root or powdered ginger
1 tbsp.	annatto seeds or 1 teaspoon turmeric
1 sprig	thyme
1	lime
	chopped parsley or basil to garnish (optional)
	salt to taste
225g (½ lb)	plain flour for dumplings/spinners (see page 67) make dumplings/spinners very small

1. Wash cow foot in luke warm water and lime juice.

2. Bring a large pan of water to the boil. Add cow foot and cook for 2 to 3 hours on low heat until tender. Skim off any bone or froth formed on top.

3. Add vegetables, dumplings and seasoning to meat. If using annatto seeds, place them in a dish. Pour over boiling water and rub with the back of a spoon until water becomes orangey/red. Pour onto meat and vegetables.

4. Bring to boil and simmer to a stew consistency.

5. Serve hot, garnished with chopped parsley or basil

Serves 6

Serve with boiled rice, rice & peas or boiled vegetables

OXTAIL J

1.5 kg (3lb)	oxtail sliced into desired thickness
225g (½ lb)	butter beans soaked overnight (You can use tinned which you do not need to soak)
1 large	onion, chopped
1	tomato, chopped
2 cloves	garlic, crushed
2 stalks	escallion or spring onion, chopped
1 small	tin of chopped tomatoes
75g (3 oz)	sweet peppers, chopped
1 tsp.	salt
1 tsp.	ground black pepper
1	whole hot pepper
1 sprig	thyme
2	bay leaves
3 tbsp	coconut or vegetable oil
1 tbsp.	lime juice

1. Wash and season oxtail with salt, ground black pepper, ginger and garlic. Leave to marinade for at least 2 hours or overnight.

2. Heat oil in frying pan or jester pot. Fry oxtail until evenly browned. Remove and set aside.

3. Sauté onion, sweet peppers, escallion and fresh tomato. Add bay leaves, oxtail and 2 pints boiling water. Simmer for approx. 2 hours or until meat is tender.

4. Stir meat, and then add butter beans, tinned tomato, thyme and whole hot pepper. Bring to the boil then cook on low heat for 10 to 15 minutes until reduced to a rich brown stew consistency.

5. Remove bay leaves, thyme and whole hot pepper before serving.

Serves 4 to 6

Serve with boiled white rice or vegetables.

POT ROAST BEEF

2.3kg (5lb)	piece of braising/chuck steak or shin of beef
2 tbsp.	wet jerk seasoning (see page 110)
1	lime, cut in half
1	lemon, cut in half
1	whole chilli pepper
1	onion, halved
2 cloves	garlic
1 sprig	fresh rosemary
1 sprig	thyme
2 stalks	escallion or spring onion
2 large	carrots, halved
3 pints	beef or vegetable stock
5 tbsp.	oil
	cornflour to thicken

1   Spread jerk seasoning over meat. Can be left overnight.

2   Heat oil in large heavy iron or jester pot. Add meat and brown on all sides.

3   Add carrots, stalks of escallion/spring onion, whole chilli pepper, onion, cloves garlic, thyme and rosemary. Add lemon and lime. Pour in stock and cover. Bring to boil. Lower heat and simmer for 2 hours or until meat is tender.

4   Remove meat. Cool and cut into slices.

5   Discard vegetables from gravy in pot. Thicken gravy with corn flour if required.

Serves 6 to 8

Serve hot with rice and peas, or boiled vegetables such as green banana, yam, sweet cassava or roasted breadfruit. Goes well with steamed cabbage or fried plantain.

FISH AND SEAFOOD DISHES

ACKEE AND SALT FISH

18	ackees or 1 large tin of ackees drained and thoroughly rinsed
450g (1lb)	salted codfish or salted mackerel (soaked overnight)
1 large	onion, chopped
2 stalks	escallion, chopped
1	fresh tomato, diced
1 small	tin tomatoes, chopped
	pinch mixed herbs
	pinch black pepper
	salt to taste
1	hot pepper deseeded and finely chopped
75g (3 oz)	sweet pepper, diced (red/yellow, green)

1. Drain off water from soaked fish. Cover fish with fresh cold water and bring to the boil. Drain off water and repeat. Place in cold water and leave to cool.

2. If using fresh ackees, remove seeds and membrane. Place ackee flesh in a pan of boiling water. Add pinch of salt and parboil for 5 minutes. Drain and put to one side.

3. Remove skin and bones from fish. Flake and put to one side.

4. Heat oil in frying pan. Add onions, escallion, fresh tomato, sweet peppers, hot pepper and sauté for 5 minutes. Add tinned tomato, mixed herbs and black pepper.

5. Stir in ackees and fish. Cook for 5 minutes until hot.

*S*erves 4

*S*erve hot with fried dumplings, boiled green banana, boiled rice or bammies.

*Y*ou can make a delicious vegetarian dish by omitting the fish.

SHRIMP AND RICE

25g (1 oz)	root ginger or ½ teaspoon powdered ginger
450g (1lb)	shrimps, boiled and shelled
2 stalks	escallion, chopped
450g (1lb)	long grain rice, boiled
1 clove	garlic, crushed
1 large	onion, chopped
1	tin chopped tomatoes
2 tbsp.	lemon juice
1 tsp.	turmeric
1 sprig	tarragon, chopped
4 tbsp.	coconut or vegetable oil
	salt and black pepper to taste
1	hot pepper, deseeded and chopped
75g (3 oz)	sweet pepper, diced (red/green/yellow)

1. Heat oil in a frying pan. Sauté peppers, escallion, onion, ginger and garlic. Add turmeric, tarragon tinned tomato and stir.
2. Add shrimps, salt and pepper to taste. Sprinkle over lemon juice and stir. Cook for 2 minutes.
3. Serve shrimps hot on a bed of rice.

Serve hot

Serves 4

Tip

According to personal taste, eggs are sometimes added to this dish.

— Add shrimps and rice to the sautéed vegetables and stir well.
— Make a hole in the centre and pour in 2 beaten eggs. Stirring all the time, until eggs are cooked and the rice dries out.
— Add salt and pepper to taste.

BARBECUED FISH

4 medium	*fish of your choice - e.g. snapper, red mullet, bream, yellow tail, jack fish Fish should be scraped and gutted, with gills and fins removed. You can ask a fishmonger to do this.*
1 tbsp.	*lemon juice*
1 tbsp.	*lime juice*
2 tbsp.	*wet or dry jerk seasoning (see page 110)*
2 tbsp.	*oil*

1. Wash fish and sprinkle with lime and lemon juice.
2. Spread jerk seasoning over each fish. Leave to marinade for at least 2 hours or overnight.
3. Brush each fish with oil on both sides.
4. Place fish on a wire rack over very hot coals and barbecue for 6 to 8 minutes on each side. Turn occasionally and brush with oil to prevent sticking.

*S*erves 4

*S*erve with barbecued vegetables, roast breadfruit, sweet potato, bammies or hard dough bread.

BARBECUED FISH & STEAMED FISH

STEAMED FISH

4 medium	fish e.g. red mullet, snapper, yellow tail, bream, goat fish. Fish should be scraped and gutted. You can ask a fishmonger to do this.
2	onions, sliced
1	whole hot pepper
50g (2 oz)	butter
6	pimento seeds or cloves
2 tbsp.	lime juice
1 sprig	thyme
1 sprig	parsley
1 sprig	rosemary
1	lemon, sliced
	salt and black pepper

1. Wash and dry fish. Core each fish by cutting two diagonal lines on each side. Rub some salt and black pepper into each cut.

2. Place fish in a deep frying pan with lid or jester pot. Add all ingredients and ½ pint water. Cover and simmer for approx. 15 minutes or until fish is tender.

OR

Place fish in foil. Add all the ingredients except water. Put fish in bamboo steamer, cover and place over saucepan of boiling water. Steam for 15 to 20 minutes or until fish is tender.

3. Remove parsley, rosemary, thyme and whole hot pepper and serve hot immediately.

Serves 4

Serve with barbecued vegetables, roast breadfruit, sweet potato, bammies or hard dough bread.

FRIED FISH

4 medium	snapper fish (or sea fish of your choice e.g. red mullet, red bream, goat fish)
1 large	onion, sliced
2 stalks	escallion or spring onion, chopped
1 tsp.	mixed herbs
1	hot pepper, deseeded and chopped
½ pint	coconut or vegetable oil
1	fennel, sliced (optional)
1 tbsp.	salt
2 tsp.	ground black pepper
5 oz	sweet peppers, sliced (red/green/yellow)
1	lime to wash fish
1	lemon
¼ lb.	flour
1 tbsp.	vinegar

1. Scale and gut fish (most fishmongers will do this for you). Wash fish with lime in a large bowl of water. Dry them on kitchen paper.

2. Core each fish by making two diagonal cuts to the bone on each side. Rub some of the salt and black pepper into cuts.

3. Mix rest of black pepper and salt with the flour. Coat each fish with mixture, knocking off any excess.

4. Heat oil in a large frying pan or jester pot.

5. Fry fish until crisp and browned on each side. Remove and drain on kitchen paper.

6. Fry onion, escallion, peppers and fennel. Stir in vinegar, mixed herbs and juice of half of the lemon. Spread over fish and serve.

7. Cut other half of the lemon into slices and garnish.

Serve hot or cold with bammies, fried dumplings, hard dough or crusty bread.

Serves 4

COOK UP LOBSTER / PRAWNS

450g (1lb)	cooked lobster meat or lobster tails
12	cooked peeled king prawns
	(or ½ lb. ordinary cooked peeled prawns)
1 large	onion, chopped
2 stalks	escallion or spring onion, chopped
1 inch piece	fresh root ginger or ½ tsp. ginger powder
½ tsp.	mixed herbs
½ tsp.	turmeric
25g (1 oz)	coconut cream
125g (4 oz)	sweet peppers, diced (red/green/yellow)
4 tbsp.	oil
1	hot pepper, deseeded and chopped
1 small	tinned tomato, chopped
1	fresh tomato, chopped
2 cloves	garlic, crushed
2	bayleaves
	salt and pepper to taste
	basil to garnish (optional)

1. Heat oil in frying pan. Add onions, escallion, peppers, fresh tomato, garlic and fry until tender.

2. Stir in mixed herbs, ginger, turmeric, coconut cream and tinned tomato. Add bay leaves and simmer for 3 minutes.

3. Add lobster meat, prawns, salt and black pepper to taste. Stir and simmer gently for a further 5 minutes. Garnish with basil (optional).

Serve hot with plain boiled rice

Serves 4

Tip

Lobster tails are much cheaper than a whole lobster.

SPICY CRAB

2	*boiled crabs*
1	*onion, chopped*
1	*hot pepper, deseeded and chopped*
2 stalks	*escallion or*
	spring onion, chopped
1 large	*fresh tomato, chopped*
¼ tsp.	*root ginger grated or*
	ginger powder
2 cloves	*garlic, crushed*
3 tbsp.	*coconut or vegetable oil*
3 tsp	*coconut milk*
1 tbsp.	*lemon juice*
1	*lemon, sliced*
	salt and pepper to taste

1. Remove meat from crab back, shells and claws. Discard gills, intestine and bits of shell. Wash crab shells well and drain.

2. Heat oil in frying pan. Add peppers, escallion, tomato, onion, garlic, ginger, fry until tender.

3. Add crabmeat, lemon juice, coconut milk, salt and pepper to taste and stir. Cook for further 5 minutes.

4. Fill each shell with crab mixture. Garnish with lemon slices.

Serves 4

Serve on a bed of lettuce leaves as a starter or with plain boiled rice as a main dish. ✓

SPICY CRAB & LOBSTER AND CRAB QUICHE

LOBSTER AND CRAB QUICHE

Filling

100g (4 oz)	cooked crabmeat - fresh or tinned
3	lobster tails, sliced (can be used instead of whole lobster and are a lot cheaper)
50g (2 oz)	sweet red pepper, diced
1 small	onion, chopped
1 small	tomato, chopped
1 clove	garlic, crushed
¼ tsp.	dried jerk seasoning (See page 110)
½ tsp.	ginger powder
½ tsp.	dried mixed herbs
2	eggs
3 tbsp.	oil
5 fl oz (¼ pint)	single cream

Pastry

225g (8 oz)	self raising flour
100g (4 oz)	butter
½ tsp.	turmeric

1. For pastry sift flour into a large bowl. Add turmeric. Rub in butter until mixture is a bread crumbs texture. Stir in approximately 3 tablespoons of cold water and mix to firm dough. Add more water if necessary. Chill for 30 minutes.

2. Put dough on a floured surface and knead lightly. Roll out and line a 10 inch fluted flan tin or 4 individual flan dishes. Prick all over with a fork and bake blind in a preheated oven for 15 minutes or until dry and lightly browned. (400°F/gas mark 6)

3. For filling, heat oil in frying pan. Fry lobster tail slices for 2 minutes until slightly browned. Remove and place on kitchen paper.

4. Add onion, pepper, tomato and garlic to frying pan. Stir in ginger powder, mixed herbs and dried jerk seasoning. Cook for 2 minutes.

5. Remove from heat and stir in crab meat.

6. Spoon mixture into flan tin or dishes.

7. Beat eggs and cream together and pour over mixture. Bake for 10 to 15 minutes or until set and golden brown.

8. Remove quiche(s) from oven. Arrange lobster tail slices on top and return to oven or preheated grill for 3 to 5 minutes or until lobster is golden brown.

Serve hot or cold with crisp salad.

MACKEREL RUN DOWN

1 large	salted mackerel (soaked over night)
1 pint	coconut milk
1 large	onion, chopped
1	hot pepper, deseeded and chopped
100g (4 oz)	sweet pepper, diced
	(red/green/yellow)
5	okra, cut into two
	(top and tail okras)
1 clove	garlic, crushed
2 stalks	escallion, chopped
4	pimento seeds or cloves
1	tomato, chopped
1 sprig	thyme
2	bay leaves
½ tsp.	ground black pepper
1 tbsp.	vinegar
1	lime, juiced
	salt to taste

MACKEREL RUN DOWN & MACKEREL WITH GREEN BANANA

1. Drain water off soaked mackerel. Place mackerel in pan of cold water and bring to boil.
    Drain and cover with cold water, leave to cool.

2. Pour coconut milk into a heavy saucepan. Lower heat and simmer for approx. 1 hour or until the milk starts to turn oily.

3. Add all other ingredients to coconut oil, except fish and hot pepper. Simmer for 5 to 7 minutes.

4. Remove bones from fish. Flake fish and add with hot pepper to coconut oil and vegetables.
    Simmer for 10 minutes. Remove hot pepper and serve.

Serve on a bed of boiled rice

Serves 4

MACKEREL WITH GREEN BANANA

2 small	*salt mackerels (soaked over night)*
8	*green bananas, peeled*
3 stalks	*escallion, chopped*
2	*hot peppers - 1 deseeded and chopped, and 1 whole*
100g (4 oz)	*sweet peppers, diced (red/green/yellow)*
50g (2 oz)	*coconut cream or 4 tablespoons coconut milk*
5 tbsp.	*coconut or vegetable oil*
1 large	*onion, chopped*
1 sprig	*thyme*
½ tsp.	*mixed herbs*
1	*lime*
½ tsp.	*ground black pepper*

1. Bring saucepan of cold water to the boil. Add coconut cream/milk and bananas. Add mackerel, 1 whole hot pepper and thyme. Simmer for 15 to 20 minutes or until bananas are tender. Turn heat down very low, to keep bananas soft. (They will go hard if water is cold). Remove mackerel from saucepan.

2. Heat oil in a frying pan. Fry sweet peppers, chopped hot pepper, escallion and onion until lightly browned. Add mixed herbs, black pepper and lime juice.

3. Cut mackerel into four pieces and place in frying pan with vegetables until heated through.

4. Remove bananas from hot water and place on serving plate with mackerel. Spread fried vegetables over mackerel and serve immediately.

Serves 4

Serve hot.

CARIBBEAN SEAFOOD KEBABS

350g (12oz)	fish, (such as bream, snapper, red mullet) filleted and cut into bite size pieces.	**Marinade**	
12 large	prawns, peeled	2	limes, juiced
1	firm mango, peeled and flesh cut into chunks from the stone	3	cloves garlic, crushed
2	firm ripe plantains, cut into chunky pieces	1	green chilli, deseeded and finely chopped
1 small	ripe pineapple cut into chunks or tinned chunks drained.	1 stalk	escallion or spring onion, chopped finely
2	sweet peppers, cubed - red, green or yellow	1 sprig	rosemary
2	sweet corn on the cob, cut into chunky slices sprigs of bay leaf lemon wedges to garnish	4 tbsp.	olive oil pinch of ground black pepper salt to taste

1. Mix marinade ingredients together. Add fish and prawns and mix well. Cover and leave to marinate in a fridge for at least 2 hours or overnight.

2. Prepare barbecue or preheat grill.

3. Arrange fish and prawns alternately on skewers with the mango, plantain, pineapple, corn, and sweet pepper. Place a bay leaf at the end of each skewer.

4. Brush with marinade.

5. Cook under grill or barbecue on grid over hot coals for 5 to 8 minutes on each side, or until cooked through. Brush with marinade whilst cooking.

6. Serve hot garnished with lemon wedges and bay leaves.

*S*erves approx. 4

*D*elicious with a variety of sauces, dips and salsa (See pages 115, 116)

Serve with salad, rice, roast breadfruit, sweet potato, sweet potato wedges, breadfruit or coconut chips

RED BREAM PASTA

450g (1 lb)	dried pasta bows (farfalle) or other dried pasta shapes
1 large	red bream, filleted and cut into bite size pieces
1 large	onion, chopped
2 stalks	escallion or spring onion, chopped
100g (4oz)	sweet peppers, diced (red/yellow/green)
1 tsp.	turmeric
2 sprigs	basil to garnish (optional)
2 tsp.	oil
25g (1oz)	butter
1	hot pepper, deseeded and chopped
½ tsp.	mixed herbs
½	lemon
2 small	bunches chives, snipped
	black pepper and salt to taste

1. Bring large saucepan of lightly salted water to the boil. Add pasta and cook for 10 to 12 minutes or as per instructions on packet.

2. Heat oil and butter in a frying pan. Add fish and fry for 2 to 3 minutes, until golden brown. Remove from oil.

3. Add sweet peppers, onion, escallion/spring onions, tomato and hot pepper to frying pan. Stir in turmeric, mixed herbs and chives. Sauté for 5 minutes.

4. Return fish to sautéed vegetables and sprinkle with lemon juice. Add salt and black pepper to taste. Stir well. Continue to cook gently for a further 2 to 3 minutes or until fish is tender.

5. Drain pasta and place into a large bowl. Toss pasta with the fish and divide into serving dishes. Garnish with basil.

Serves 4

VEGETABLE DISHES

RICE AND PEAS

225g (½ lb)	kidney beans (or gungo peas, black eye peas or sam gale french beans)
	milk from one fresh coconut or ½ tin coconut milk
	or 4 oz coconut cream
2	whole stalks escallion or spring onions
1 sprig	fresh thyme
1	whole hot pepper
900g (2 lb)	long grain rice
2 tsp.	salt

1. If using dried peas (except black eyed peas) soak overnight in cold water.

2. Place peas in a large saucepan and cover with cold water. Cover and bring to the boil. Simmer until peas are tender.

3. Add coconut milk, salt, whole stalks escallion/spring onion, thyme and whole hot pepper. Bring to boil, add rice and stir. Make sure that the water is just covering the rice (too much water will make it soggy). Reduce to very low heat and simmer for 30 minutes or until rice is tender and water is absorbed. If rice remains hard add a little amount of water if necessary and simmer until cooked.

4. Remove whole pepper, escallion and thyme and stir.

Serve hot

Serves 6

Traditionally served with chicken as a Sunday dinner. Can also be served with curried goat, pork and beef dishes.

TURNED CORNMEAL ✓

450g (1lb)	cornmeal
100g (4 oz)	sweet peppers, diced (red/yellow/green)
2	fresh tomatoes, chopped
2 stalks	escallion or spring onion, chopped
1	hot pepper, deseeded and chopped
1 pint	coconut milk
1	onion, chopped
½ tsp.	mixed herbs
½ tsp.	salt
½ tsp.	ground black pepper
2 tbsp.	coconut or vegetable oil

1. Heat oil in a heavy saucepan or jester pot.
2. Sauté onion, escallion/spring onion, peppers, and tomatoes. Add mixed herbs, black pepper, salt and stir.
3. Add coconut milk and bring to the boil. Lower heat and sprinkle in cornmeal. Stir briskly with a wooden spoon.
4. Turn heat very low, cover and cook for approx. 25 minutes, or until milk is absorbed and cornmeal is cooked. Stir occasionally during cooking.

Serve on its own or as a side dish with meat or fish.

Can also be chilled in the fridge to make it more solid. Then cut into slices and fried.

JOHNNY CAKES/FRIED DUMPLINGS

775g (1½ lbs)   self-raising flour
                   (or plain flour with a teaspoon of baking powder)
25g (1 oz)   margarine or butter
½ tsp.   salt
300ml (½ pint)   oil
                   water to make dough

1. Rub flour, salt and margarine in a large bowl, then add water to form a soft dough.
2. Divide dough into about 12 small balls. Knead each one from the outside in for ½ minute.
3. Heat oil in a large deep frying or heavy pan.
4. Press each ball down with the palm of your hand and place in hot oil.
5. Cover with a lid and lower the heat. Fry for 3-4 minutes then turn onto the other side. Cook gently until golden brown.
6. Remove from oil and rest on kitchen paper to drain.

Serve hot or cold.

Can be served as a snack or with fish, meat, ackee and other vegetable dishes.

Tip

Sugar and nutmeg/cinnamon can be added to serve as a sweet dish.
Use the same process but make the balls smaller.

DUMPLINGS/SPINNERS

450g (1 lb)   Plain flour
½ tsp.   Salt

1. Sift flour and salt.
2. Add enough cold water to make stiff dough.
3. Knead dough for about 5 minutes.

DUMPLINGS

1. Divide dough into balls approx. 1½ inches in diameter. Knead each one, and flatten.
2. Drop dumplings into boiling water or into soup or stew and cook for 15 to 20 minutes.

   Makes 12 to 14 dumplings

SPINNERS

1. Roll dough in palm of your hand into sausage shapes. (approx. 2½ inches long and ½ inch thick).
2. Drop spinners into soup or stew.

DROP SPOON DUMPLINGS

1. Sift flour and salt
2. Add water and stir with a wooden spoon to make stiff dough.
3. Fill a tablespoon with some of the dough and drop into boiling water, stew or soup
   Repeat process until dough finished.

   Makes approx.16 dumplings.

CASSAVA HEAD DUMPLINGS

450g (1lb)	Plain flour
450g (1lb)	Cassava
½ tsp.	Salt

1. Scrape skin from cassava, then grate or cut into small pieces and put in blender.
2. Put cassava in muslin cloth or tea towel, and wring out juice.
3. Rub cassava into breadcrumb texture.
4. Sift cassava and add to flour and salt.
5. Add water to make firm dough.
6. Knead and divide into approx. 9 balls.
7. Knead each ball and flatten with palm of hand.
8. Place into boiling water or soup.
9. Cook for 15 to 20 minutes.
   (Dumplings will sink to the bottom of the pot when cooked)

CORNMEAL DUMPLINGS

450g (1lb)	Plain flour
100g (4 oz)	Cornmeal
½ tsp.	Salt

1. Sift flour and salt. Add cornmeal.
2. Add water and mix into a stiff dough. Follow same procedure as above for cooking.

GREEN BANANA DUMPLINGS

450g (1lb)	Plain flour
½ tsp.	Salt
3	Green bananas

1. Peel bananas and grate or cut into small pieces and place in blender.
2. Sift flour and salt. Add banana. Follow same procedure as above for cooking.

These dumplings can be boiled on their own or with vegetables. Traditionally they are cooked with certain soups. These include pepperpot, peas, vegetable, pumpkin and spinach/calloo soups. They are not usually cooked in mannish water or beef soup, for which plain dumplings, spinners or drop spoon dumplings are used.

ROAST BREADFRUIT

The skin of the breadfruit used for roasting should be brownish in colour, and the flesh inside a yellowish white. This is known as a ' fit' breadfruit. Tinned breadfruit or a fresh breadfruit with green skin is not suitable for roasting, but can be used for boiling or for soup.

2	whole 'fit' breadfruits
1 tbsp.	salt
50g (2 oz)	butter

Roasted over open flame

1. Remove the stem and pierce through the core of the breadfruit with a sharp knife.
2. Place breadfruit on grid over hot coals.
3. Turn breadfruit as each section of the skin blackens.
4. Once the skin of the breadfruit is black all over, remove and leave to cool.
5. Peel off the skin. Cut the breadfruit into segments and remove the core.
6. Cut into slices and serve.
7. Spread with butter and sprinkle with salt to taste, if desired.

In the oven

1. Prick the skin of the breadfruit all over and rub in the salt and butter.
2. Wrap in foil and place in preheated oven (375°F/ gas mark 5) for approx. 2 hours or until cooked. You can test if it is cooked by sticking a clean knife into it, and if knife comes out clean the breadfruit is ready.
3. Peel off the skin of the breadfruit. Cut into segments and remove the core.
4. Cut into slices of desired thickness and serve.

Roast breadfruit is usually served with fish and meat dishes. It can be served with or instead of rice, or vegetables.

STUFFED BREADFRUIT

1. Roast the breadfruit as above and cut into two halves.
2. Remove the core and fill each half with filling of your choice e.g. shrimps/prawns/crab, ackee and salt fish, run down, spinach/callaloo etc.

Serve hot

SWEET POTATO AU GRATIN

450g (1lb)	sweet potatoes
100g (4oz)	sweet peppers, sliced (red/yellow/green)
175g (6oz)	cheddar cheese, grated
2 stalks	escallion or spring onions
¼ tsp.	mixed herbs
¼ tsp.	saffron or turmeric
¼ pint	coconut milk
2 tbsp.	oil
2	vegetable stock cubes
	salt to taste
	ground black pepper to taste
	parsley to garnish (optional)

1. Boil sweet potatoes in salted water. Cook for approx.15 minutes. Drain and leave to cool.

2. Heat oil in a frying pan. Fry sweet pepper and escallion. Add saffron/ turmeric and mixed herbs. Stir and remove from heat.

3. Peel and cut sweet potato into thick slices.

4. Arrange sweet potato, sweet peppers and escallion in layers in a greased ovenproof dish, seasoning each layer with salt and ground black pepper.

5. Mix coconut milk and stock cubes together. Pour over the vegetables.

6. Sprinkle the cheese all over.

7. Bake in a preheated oven (400°F/gas mark 6) for 30 minutes, or until golden. Garnish with parsley and serve.

*S*erves 4

AUBERGINE AND CALLALOO BAKE

3 medium	aubergines (garden egg)
450g (1lb)	callaloo leaves, chopped (can use spinach leaves, chopped)
1 small	tin sweet corn, drained
1	onion, diced
100g (4 oz)	sweet peppers, diced
2 stalks	escallion, chopped
½	scotch bonnet pepper, deseeded and finely chopped
3	tomatoes, chopped
175g (6 oz)	cheddar cheese, grated
1 small	tinned tomato, chopped
4 tbsp.	oil
1 sprig	basil, chopped
½ tsp.	ground black pepper
½ tsp.	salt

1. Slice aubergines and place in salt water for 3 minutes. Rinse and pat dry.

2. Heat 3 tablespoons of the oil in a large frying pan. Add aubergines and fry until lightly browned on each side. Place on kitchen towel to drain.

3. Add remaining oil to frying pan. Fry callaloo, onion, fresh tomato and peppers. Add tinned tomato, sweet corn, scotch bonnet pepper, basil, black pepper and salt to taste.

4. Layer aubergine and other vegetables in an ovenproof dish.

5. Sprinkle over cheese. Bake in preheated oven (375°F/gas mark 5) for 30 minutes or until golden brown.

Serves 4

Serve hot with plain boiled rice, fried dumplings, roti, crusty or hard dough bread.

CALLALOO

900g (2 lbs)	callaloo or spinach leaves, chopped
1	onion, chopped
3 stalks	escallion or spring onions, chopped
1	hot pepper, deseeded and chopped
1 sprig	thyme
50ml (2 fl oz)	coconut milk
1 large	tin tomatoes, chopped
1 clove	garlic, crushed
4 tbsp.	coconut or vegetable oil
½ tsp.	salt
¼ tsp.	ground black pepper

1. Blanch callaloo in salted boiling water for 3 minutes. Remove from water. If you are using spinach there is no need to blanch it.

2. Heat oil in frying pan. Sauté onions, pepper, thyme and escallion. Add garlic, tinned tomato, coconut milk and stir. Simmer for 4 minutes.

3. Add callaloo or spinach, black pepper, salt to taste and stir well. Simmer for a further 3 minutes or unti callaloo/spinach is cooked. Remove thyme and serve.

Serves 4

This dish is idea for vegetarians. However, in Jamaica it is usually served with salt fish, and pieces of fried pork. This is accompanied with boiled green bananas, bammy, roast breadfruit, fried dumplings or boiled rice, as a late Sunday breakfast or main meal during the week.

BOILED VEGETABLES

In Jamaica there are a variety of starchy vegetables that usually accompany main dishes. They can be served with or instead of rice. The main ones are, yam, sweet potato, sweet cassava, green banana, breadfruit, coco, plantain and dasheen. All these vegetables are available in Jamaican and Asian stores. There is some availability in large stores.

To get the real taste of Jamaica and traditional authentic cuisine, these vegetables put the finishing touches to your meal. Whilst some of them can simply be boiled like potato, others require certain procedures in cooking.

Breadfruit

Breadfruit is not edible until cooked. In Jamaica they are very much enjoyed roasted (page 69).

To boil – peel skin, cut into segments and remove core.
Cut into thick slices and boil until tender.
Usually added to stews and soups to enhance flavour.
Can be fried into chips (page 17).

Breadfruit can now be obtained in tins, this makes a good substitute if serving boiled, or in stews and soups.

Coco

Peel the skin, and boil for approx. 10 to 15 minutes.
They are usually added to stews and soups.
You can also use them instead of potatoes.

Dasheen

Similar to coco, but much bigger in size. Peel skin and cut into small pieces.
Boil and serve as a vegetable or add to stews or soups.

Green Bananas

Much firmer than ripe bananas and skin is green. Remove skins by coring side and peeling back, then place in boiling water. Simmer for 10 to 15 minutes or until tender. Add 1oz of butter or coconut cream to bring out the flavour and keep their colour. If not served immediately, they should be kept in hot water, otherwise they will go hard and discoloured.

Plantain

Looks similar to a banana, but is much larger. However, plantains must be cooked before eating. Cooking depends on stage of ripeness. Green plantains are usually boiled in their skin until tender. Skin is then removed, and plantain served hot with main dishes. Green plantains are also used for plantain chips (page 17).

Ripe plantains can be cooked in various ways. Steam or boil them in their skins. Make sure they are ripe but firm. Cook until they are tender. Remove skin and serve with meat, fish and vegetable dishes such as ackee, spinach/callaloo. Ripe plantains are a favourite when fried. Simply remove skin, cut into slices lengthways and fry in shallow oil. Delicious served with ackee and salt fish, bacon and eggs, ham etc. Crush ripe plantain and add to batter mix for fritters.

They can be baked in their skins; to accompany main dishes or as a sweet ingredient added to produce a pudding.

Sweet cassava

Usually boiled and served as a main vegetable. Peel the rough skin and white rind. Cut into pieces, and place in boiling water. Simmer until soft. Goes very well in soups.

Sweet cassava is also used to make traditional bammy (see page 80).

Sweet potato

Can be boiled, baked or fried like normal potatoes. Parboil and dry thoroughly before frying.

Enhance their flavour by boiling and mashing them, then add butter and mixed herbs.

Delicious as a snack made into seasoned wedges (page 26)

Used in one of Jamaica's best-loved sweets - sweet potato pudding (page 94)

Yam

One of the most widely used vegetables in Jamaica. White and yellow yams are freely available and commonly used.

Peel skin and cut into thick slices or chunks. They can be cooked in the same way as potatoes – boiled, roasted or baked.
You can mash them like potatoes, add butter and mixed herbs.

Yam goes well with most dishes. It has a texture similar to potato, but has a distinctive nutlike flavour. Adds richness to soups, stews, and vegetable dishes.

BREADS

HARD DOUGH BREAD

900g (2lb) self-raising flour
1 tbsp.   dried yeast
50g (2 oz) butter
3 tbsp.   granulated sugar
1 tsp.   salt

1. Sprinkle the yeast and 1 teaspoon of the sugar over ½ pint of hand hot water. Cover with cling film and leave until it froths.

2. Sift flour and salt in a large bowl. Add the rest of the sugar and cut in the butter.

3. Add yeast mixture and knead for about 10 to 15 minutes into a firm dough.

4. Place dough in a greased bowl. Turn it over to make sure it is coated with the oil.

5. Cover with a warm damp cloth and leave to double in size.

6. Turn dough out on to a lightly floured surface. Knead and roll into rectangles and put into two 2lb (900g) loaf tins.

7. Cover with a damp tea towel and leave to rise to nearly fill tin.

8. Bake in a preheated oven (400°F/gas mark 7) for 30 to 40 minutes. The bread should have a firm texture.

9. Turn out on wire rack to cool.

CORN BREAD ✓

175g (6oz)	fine cornmeal
50g (2 oz)	self raising flour
1 tsp.	baking powder
50g (2 oz)	butter, melted
1 tsp.	salt
8 fl oz	milk
2	eggs, beaten
25g (1 oz)	sugar
1 tsp.	pumpkin or poppy seeds (optional)

1. Put all dry ingredients in a large bowl.
2. Mix together butter, milk and eggs. Pour on to dry ingredients and mix well to a batter consistency.
3. Pour batter into a greased 8 inch square tin. Bake in a preheated oven (375°F/gas mark 5) for 25 to 30 minutes or until light gold in colour. Insert a skewer or knife in the centre, and if it comes out clean the bread is done.
4. Leave in tin for several minutes, then turn out on a wire rack to cool.

Serve warm on its own with butter or with savoury meat and fish dishes.

PUMPKIN BREAD

450g (1 lb)	plain flour
1 tbsp.	dried yeast
1 tsp.	sugar
1 tbsp.	golden syrup
225g (8 oz)	pumpkin
1 tsp.	salt
25g (1 oz)	butter
1 tbsp.	pumpkin seeds
1	egg yolk beaten with
1 tbsp	milk for glazing

1. Remove seeds from pumpkin and put in a saucepan to cook.
2. Sift flour and salt in a large bowl.
3. Sprinkle yeast and sugar over ½ pint hand hot water. Cover and leave for 5 minutes or until it froths.
4. Remove pumpkin from water, peel off the skin and mash with the butter. Leave to cool.
5. Make a well in the flour.
6. Stir golden syrup into yeast mixture. Pour into the well in the flour.
7. Add pumpkin and mix to soft dough. Adding a little water if necessary.
8. Turn dough out onto a lightly floured surface and knead for about 5 minutes.
9. Put dough into a greased bowl, cover with a warm damp towel and leave to double in size.
10. Put dough on a lightly floured surface and knead in the pumpkin seeds.
11. Divide dough into 2 equal pieces, knead until smooth. Place into 2 loaf tins and cover with a damp tea towel. Leave to nearly double in size.
12. Brush the loaves with egg yolk and milk mixture.
13. Bake in a preheated oven (425°F/gas mark 7) for about 30 minutes or until golden brown and shrunk from the sides of the tins. The base of the bread will sound hollow when tapped.
14. Turn out and cool on a wire rack. Makes two loaves.

Serve warm or cold. Delicious with soup.

ROTI

450g (1 lb)	self-raising flour
½ tsp.	salt
8 fl oz	coconut milk
2 tbsp.	oil or 2 oz butter

1. Mix ingredients to form dough.
2. Divide into balls approx. 2 inches in diameter. Roll each one out to approx. ½ inch thickness on a floured surface.
3. Brush with melted butter or oil, and place in a heated heavy frying pan or jester pot. Cook until browned on that side.
4. Brush the other side with butter or oil, and turn roti over.
5. Press lightly on roti whilst each side is cooking.
6. When browned on each side remove and serve hot.

Makes approx. 12 roti

Serve with most meat and fish dishes.

SPICY COCONUT ROTI

350g (12 oz)	self raising flour
100g (4 oz)	cornmeal
75g (3 oz)	grated coconut or desiccated coconut
½ tsp.	salt
½ tsp.	chilli powder
25g (1 oz)	escallion or spring onion, finely chopped
2 tbsp.	oil or butter
25g (1 oz)	butter, melted
2 tbsp.	marjoram, finely chopped
¼ tsp.	freshly ground black pepper
8 fl oz.	coconut milk

1. Mix flour, cornmeal, coconut, salt, chilli powder and black pepper in a bowl.
2. Coat the escallion/spring onion and marjoram in the melted butter. Add to the flour mixture.
3. Stir in the coconut milk to make stiff dough.
4. Divide and make into roti as above.

Serve with jerk or barbecued meats or fried fish. Delicious with chutneys.

BAMMY/ CASSAVA BREAD

2.3kg (5 lb) cassava

pinch salt

1. Scrape skin off cassava.
2. Grate cassava or cut into small pieces and place in a blender.
3. Place in a muslin cloth or strong tea towel, press and wring out all the juice into a dish. The cassava must be as dry as possible.
4. Leave juice in dish to settle for at least 1 hour. Strain liquid off and mix starchy mixture in bottom of dish with cassava.
5. Put cassava on a tray to dry out for at least 2 hours.
6. When dry rub cassava into a bread crumbs texture.
7. Sift cassava to remove rough pieces.
8. Add salt to taste
9. Heat a small heavy frying pan or jester pot.
10. Sprinkle enough cassava to thinly cover the bottom of the frying pan/jester pot.
11. Press down lightly all over mixture with a tea towel, or the bottom of a cup until mixture is firm and the edges shrink from sides of pan. Turn over and repeat process. Bammy should be lightly browned.
12. Repeat process until mixture is finished.

This is a recipe for thin bammies. You can buy thick bammies ready made.

1. Soak them in milk or water for 5 minutes.
2. Cover with cling film and microwave for no longer than 2 minutes to soften them.
3. They can also be toasted or fried in shallow oil before serving.

Serve hot or cold

Traditionally served with fried fish. Can also be served with meat, vegetable dishes such as ackee, spinach/callaloo.
Cut into wedges and serve with soup.
Bammies can be reheated, toasted and fried.
They can also be frozen.
If bammies become dry, sprinkle with water before warming.

WATER CRACKERS

175g (6 oz)	plain flour
1 tsp.	baking powder
25g (1 oz)	butter
50ml (2 fl oz)	water
½ tsp.	salt

1. Sift flour, baking powder and salt into a bowl.
2. Rub in butter. Add water and mix to dough.
3. Turn out onto a lightly floured surface. Knead until smooth.
4. Roll out thinly and prick with a fork.
5. Cut out with a 3½ inch plain cutter.
6. Place on greased baking sheets.
7. Bake in a preheated oven (350ºF/gas mark 4) for approx. 15 minutes, or until cooked through and slightly brown in colour.
8. Cool on a wire rack.

*M*akes approximately 20 crackers.

*S*erve with paté, cheese, fried sprats or sardines, Solomon Gundy. Many Jamaicans like to dunk them in coffee.

COCO BREAD

1¼ lb.	plain flour
1 sachet	yeast
6 oz	butter
1 tsp.	sugar
3 fl. oz	warm water
6 fl. oz	warm milk
2	eggs, beaten
1 tsp.	salt

1. Dissolve the yeast and sugar in the warm water and leave for 5 minutes.
2. Add milk and eggs to yeast mixture and stir well.
3. Put flour and salt in a large bowl.
4. Stir in yeast mixture to form dough.
5. Turn dough onto a floured surface and knead until firm (about 10 minutes).
6. Put dough into a well-greased bowl.
7. Cover with cling film or a warm damp towel. Leave to rise until doubled in size.
8. Turn dough onto a floured surface and knead for approximately 5 minutes.
9. Cut dough into 10 portions.
10. Roll each portion into a circle approximately 6 inches in diameter.
11. Melt butter and brush each circle.
12. Fold each circle in half and brush again with butter. Repeat this process once more to form triangle shapes.
13. Place on a greased baking sheet, on a baking tray. Leave to rise until doubled in size.
14. Half fill a large pan or baking tray with hot water and place on the bottom shelf of a preheated oven (425°F/gas mark 8).
15. Place baking tray with breads on the top shelf and bake for approximately 15 minutes or until golden brown.
16. Remove and leave on a wire rack to cool.

Serve hot or cold.

Usually eaten any time of the day with most dishes, or as a snack with cheese, hot chocolate or coffee.

CAKES AND PUDDINGS

JAMAICAN BUN

450g (1lb)	plain flour
2 tsp.	baking powder
100g (4 oz)	butter or margarine
100g (4 oz)	raisins
100g (4 oz)	currants
50g (2 oz)	mixed peel
1	egg
350g (12oz)	brown sugar
2 tbsp.	honey
1 tsp.	cinnamon
1 tsp.	nutmeg
	milk to bind into dough
2 tbsp.	sugar for glaze

1. Cream butter/margarine and sugar. Beat in eggs and add honey.
2. Sift flour, baking powder, cinnamon and nutmeg. Add dried fruits, butter and sugar mixture and mix well.
3. Add milk to make into soft dough.
4. Turn onto a floured surface and knead for few minutes.
5. Place into a greased loaf tin. Bake in preheated oven at 350 °F/gas mark 4, for approximately 1 hour or until cooked through.
6. Make a glaze of 2 tablespoons of sugar boiled with water, and brush over warm bun.

Serves approx. 10 slices.

Usually served buttered with cheese.

BULLA CAKES

450g (1lb)	self raising flour
1 tsp.	baking powder
½ tsp.	bicarbonate of soda
225g (8 oz)	wet sugar or dark brown sugar
50ml (2 fl oz)	water
2 tbsp.	melted butter
1 tsp.	ground ginger
¼ tsp.	salt
1 tsp.	cinnamon
½ tsp.	nutmeg

1. If using dark brown sugar instead of wet sugar, make a syrup of the sugar and water.
2. Sift together dry ingredients.
3. Add syrup and melted butter. Mix well to form a soft dough.
4. Turn on to a floured board and knead for about 3 to 4 minutes.
5. Roll out to ½ inch thickness. Cut into circles by using a saucer or large glass.
6. Grease and slightly flour a baking tray.
7. Place bullas on tray and bake in preheated oven for 20 minutes, 400°F/gas mark 6.
8. As an option bullas can be brushed with melted butter whilst warm.

Makes approx. 8 bullas.

In Jamaica bullas are eaten on their own, or with slices of avocado pear and slices of tinned processed cheese.

BULLA CAKES & JAMAICAN BUN

JAMAICAN RUM CAKE

8 tbsp.
dark or white Jamaican rum
300ml (½ pint)   sherry
175g (6 oz)   plain flour
1 ½ tsp.   baking powder
225g (8 oz)   soft brown sugar
½ tsp.   mixed spice
½ tsp.   vanilla
½ tsp.   cinnamon
4   eggs
100g (4 oz)   butter or margarine
2 tsp.   molasses or gravy browning
                   pinch of salt

1. Cream butter, sugar and eggs. Stir in rum and vanilla.
2. Sift flour and baking powder. Add mixed spice, cinnamon and salt. Fold this into the butter and sugar mixture and mix well.
3. Stir in sherry and molasses or gravy browning.
4. Spoon cake mixture into a greased 7-inch cake tin.
5. Bake in a preheated oven (350°F/gas mark 4) for 1 hour or until a skewer inserted in the centre comes out clean.
6. Leave cake to completely cool in the tin before removing.

PINEAPPLE CAKE

1 small   tin of pineapple, drained and crushed
175g (6 oz)   plain flour
1 ½ tsp.   baking powder
100g (4 oz)   butter or margarine
225g (8 oz)   soft brown sugar
1   egg
½ tsp.   nutmeg
½ tsp.   cinnamon
½ tsp.   vanilla
                   pinch of salt

1. Cream butter, eggs and sugar.
2. Sift flour and baking powder. Add salt, cinnamon and nutmeg. Stir into butter and sugar mixture. Stir in pineapple and vanilla.
3. Pour cake mixture into a 7 inch cake or loaf tin.
4. Bake in a preheated oven (350°F/ gas mark 4) for 1 hour or until a skewer inserted in the middle comes out clean.
5. Leave in the tin for 10 minutes then turn out onto a wire rack to cool completely.

BANANA CAKE

1	*ripe banana, crushed*
100g (4 oz)	*butter or margarine*
225g (8 oz)	*self raising flour*
1 tsp.	*baking powder*
175g (6 oz)	*soft brown sugar*
2	*eggs*
3 tbsp.	*milk*
½ tsp.	*vanilla*
½ tsp.	*nutmeg*
½ tsp.	*ginger, grated or ginger powder*
	pinch of salt

1. Cream sugar, butter and eggs. Stir in crushed banana and vanilla, mix well.

2. Sift flour and baking powder. Add nutmeg, cinnamon and ginger. Fold into sugar and butter mixture. Stir in milk.

3. Turn cake mixture into a greased loaf tin or 7 inch cake tin.

4. Bake in a preheated oven (350°F/gas mark 4) for 1 hour or until a skewer inserted in the middle comes out clean.

5. Leave in tin for 10 minutes then turn out onto a wire rack to finish cooling.

GINGER CAKE

3 tsp.	*ground ginger*
275g (10 oz)	*plain flour*
1½ tsp.	*bicarbonate of soda*
175g (6 oz)	*butter or margarine*
175g (6 oz)	*soft brown sugar*
100g (4 oz)	*molasses or black treacle*
100g (4 oz)	*golden syrup*
2	*eggs*
1 tsp.	*mixed spice*
4 fl. oz	*milk*

1. Sift flour into a large bowl. Add bicarbonate of soda, mixed spice and ginger.

2. Melt sugar, butter, syrup and molasses/black treacle in a large saucepan over a low heat.

3. Beat eggs and milk together. Make a well in the middle of the flour and add milk mixture. Fold in flour from sides of bowl to the centre.

4. Gradually stir in syrup mixture.

5. Pour mixture into greased lined or floured 9-inch cake tin or deep roasting tin.

6. Bake in a preheated oven (350°F/gas mark 4) for 1 hour.

7. Leave to cool in tin, then turn out on a wire rack. Cut into desired square portions or slices to serve.

RICH FRUIT CAKE

225g (8 oz)	self-raising flour
225g (8 oz)	raisins
225g (8 oz)	currants
225g (8 oz)	sultanas
100g (4 oz)	mixed peel
100g (4 oz)	glacé cherries, quartered
200g (7 oz)	dark brown sugar
225g (8 oz)	butter
1 tbsp.	molasses or black treacle
4	eggs
1 tsp.	mixed spice
1 tsp.	vanilla
300ml (½ pint)	sherry
8 tbsp.	dark rum
2	oranges, rind grated

1. Soak raisins, currants, sultanas, mixed peel and cherries in the rum and sherry for at least 2 weeks, preferably longer. Jar or container should have an airtight lid. Stir and add more alcohol if desired during soaking.

2. Grease and line an 8 inch round or 7 inch square cake tin with greaseproof paper.

3. Cream butter, sugar and molasses/treacle until light and fluffy. Beat in eggs.

4. Sift flour and add mixed spices. Stir into the butter and sugar mixture.

5. Stir in fruit mixture, orange rind and vanilla. Mix well adding rum or sherry if required.

6. Turn cake mixture into prepared tin. Bake in a preheated oven (350°F/gas mark 4) for 1 hour. Reduce temperature to 275°F/gas mark 1 for a further 1½ hours or until cake is cooked through. Use a skewer to test if cake is cooked by inserting it in the centre of the cake. If skewer comes out clean, the cake is cooked.

7. Leave cake in tin to cool. If not using immediately, wrap in foil when cold and store in a cool dry place to keep it moist. It will last for up to 3 months,

8. During storage prick surface of the cake and sprinkle with rum.

COCONUT CRUNCHIES

100g (4 oz)	desiccated coconut
50g (2 oz)	ground almonds
100g (4 oz)	butter (unsalted)
100g (4 oz)	soft brown sugar
100g (4 oz)	plain flour
½ tsp.	vanilla
½ tsp.	cinnamon
	pinch of salt

1. Beat sugar and butter until light and fluffy. Stir in vanilla.
2. Sift flour, salt and cinnamon into a bowl. Add ground almonds and 3 oz of the coconut.
3. Mix with butter and sugar mixture to form dough. Knead lightly.
4. Shape dough into a roll approximately 7½ inch long. Wrap in cling film and put in fridge for at least 4 hours or over night.
5. Grease several baking sheets with butter.
6. Cut the dough into slices approx. ¼ inch thickness.
7. Place slices on baking sheets.
8. Bake in a preheated oven (350 °F/gas mark 4) for 15 to 20 minutes or until lightly browned.
9. Remove biscuits from oven and sprinkle over remaining coconut whilst hot.
10. Place on wire racks to cool.

*M*akes approx. 30 biscuits.

SWEET SPICE BISCUITS

100g (4 oz)	soft brown sugar
100g (4 oz)	butter
225g (8 oz)	plain flour
1	egg, beaten
½ tsp.	baking powder
¼ tsp.	mixed spice
½ tsp	ground ginger
¼ tsp.	ground cloves
¼ tsp.	vanilla
For glaze	
6 tsp.	granulated sugar
1	egg, beaten
2 tsp.	castor sugar
3 tsp.	milk

1. Sift flour, spices, baking powder and salt in a large bowl. Stir in sugar.
2. Rub in butter, until mixture resembles breadcrumbs. Stir in egg to form dough.
3. Roll out dough on a floured surface to $1/8$-inch thickness.
4. Using desired shape cutters, cut out shapes. Use as much of the dough as possible by re kneading and re rolling trimmings.
5. Grease several baking sheets with butter.
6. Place shapes in fridge for 30 minutes.
7. Make glaze by stirring together castor sugar, egg and milk.
8. Brush each shape with glaze. Sprinkle half amount of granulated sugar over the shapes.
9. Bake in a preheated oven (350ºF/gas mark 4) for 15 to 20 minutes or until lightly browned.
10. Sprinkle over remaining granulated sugar whilst hot.
11. Remove from baking sheets and place on wire racks to cool.

*M*akes approx. 30 biscuits.

GINGER BISCUITS

2 tsp.	*ground ginger*
225g (8 oz)	*plain flour*
225g (8 oz)	*brown sugar*
100g (4 oz)	*margarine*
1	*egg*
2 tbsp.	*golden syrup or honey*
1 tsp.	*bicarbonate of soda*

1. Sift flour, bicarbonate of soda and ginger. Rub in margarine until mixture resembles breadcrumbs. Stir in sugar.
2. Make a well in the centre of the mixture, and drop in egg and golden syrup/honey. Mix well into a dough.
3. Grease several baking sheets.
4. Roll dough into walnut size balls. Place on baking sheets about 3 inches apart. Flatten each ball slightly.
5. Bake in preheated oven (350ºF/gas mark 4) for 15 to 20 minutes until golden brown.
6. Remove from baking sheets after a few minutes and place on wire racks to harden and cool.

Makes approx. 30 biscuits.

COCONUT AND TROPICAL FRUIT PUDDING ✓

50g (2 oz)	fresh grated coconut (or desiccated)
2 small	bananas, sliced
4	pineapple rings, cut into pieces (fresh or tinned)
½	tin guava halves, chopped
1 small	ripe mango, peeled, stoned and cubed
175g (6 oz)	self raising flour
½ tsp.	mixed spice
175g (6 oz)	caster sugar
175g (6 oz)	butter or margarine
3	eggs, beaten
3 tbsp.	dark rum (optional)

Serves 6

1. Cream butter and sugar. Gradually add eggs and rum.
2. Sift flour and baking powder. Fold flour and coconut into butter and sugar mixture. Mix well.
2. Place fruits into an 8-inch lightly greased ovenproof dish. Sprinkle over mixed spice.
3. Cover with sponge mix.
4. Bake in a preheated oven (350° F/gas mark 4) for 25 to 30 minutes or until sponge is golden and springs back to the touch.
5. Loosen edges of the sponge with a flat knife. Cover dish with a large plate and turn out pudding.

Serve warm with custard, double cream or ice cream.

MANGO AND ORANGE CHEESECAKE

150g (5 oz)	ginger biscuit crumbs
50g (2 oz)	butter
1 large tin	mango slices in syrup
25g (1 oz)	dark brown sugar
450g (1lb)	curd cheese
50g (2 oz)	castor sugar
3	oranges, juiced and rind grated
10g (½ oz)	gelatine
8 fl oz	single cream
	pinch of nutmeg
	pinch of cinnamon
5 fl oz	whipping cream to decorate

Serves 8

1. Melt butter in a saucepan. Stir in brown sugar, cinnamon, nutmeg and biscuit crumbs.
2. Spread and press biscuit mixture into an 8-inch loose- bottom cake tin. Place in fridge.
3. Beat curd cheese, castor sugar and rind of the oranges in a bowl.
4. Roughly chop half tin of mango slices and add to curd cheese.
5. Add the juice of the oranges to the mixture. Stir in single cream.
6. Sprinkle gelatine over 3 tablespoons of water in a small bowl. Stand the bowl in hot water and stir until gelatine dissolved.
7. Stir gelatine into cheese mixture. Pour over the biscuit base. Return to fridge to set for 2 to 3 hours.
8. Remove from tin and place on serving plate.
9. To decorate arrange remaining mango slices over surface and pipe with whipped cream around the edge.

TIE-A-LEAF
(BLUE DRAWERS/DUCKANOO)

450g (1lb)	cornmeal
175g (6 oz)	self-raising flour
350g (12 oz)	brown sugar
1 pint	coconut milk
1 small	fresh coconut grated or
	6 oz desiccated coconut
2 tsp.	vanilla
½ tsp.	mixed spice
½ tsp.	nutmeg
2 tbsp.	golden syrup or molasses
100g (4 oz)	butter or margarine
½ tsp.	ginger, grated
1 tsp.	salt
½ tsp.	cinnamon
2	banana leaves (optional)
	string or aluminium foil

TIE-A-LEAF & SWEET POTATO PUDDING

1. Mix all dry ingredients and grated coconut thoroughly.
2. Mix together coconut milk, vanilla, and golden syrup or molasses. Add to dry ingredients and stir briskly.
3. Place banana leaves over an open flame or over boiling water. Remove from centre and cut leaves into large rectangles.
4. Put a generous amount of mixture on each rectangle. Fold sides of banana leaf and tie with string into parcels. You can use aluminium foil instead of banana leaves.
5. Drop parcels into enough boiling water to cover them. Simmer for 40 minutes, or until solid.

*D*elicious hot or cold on its own or with cream.

*I*n Jamaica this boiled pudding is usually served for breakfast, light lunch or a snack.

SWEET POTATO PUDDING

1½ lb	sweet potato, peeled and grated
½ lb	cornmeal
1 large	egg
1 pint	milk
½ lb	brown sugar
4 oz	self raising flour
1 tsp.	mixed spice
½ tsp.	nutmeg
½ tsp.	ginger powder
6 oz	fresh coconut, grated (you can use desiccated)
½	tin evaporated milk
3 tbsp.	golden syrup
1 tsp.	vanilla
½ tsp.	cinnamon
	pinch of salt

1. Mix sweet potato, flour, cornmeal, coconut and sugar. Add mixed spice, ginger, cinnamon, nutmeg, vanilla and stir.

2. Add egg, golden syrup, evaporated milk and salt. Mix briskly with a wooden spoon. Pour mixture into a greased small jester pot or 8-inch tin.

3. Bake in oven for 1 to 1½ hours (375°F/gas mark 5). You can check if it is cooked by sticking a clean knife in the centre of the pudding. If it comes out clean remove from oven, and leave to cool.

4. Cut into thick slices and serve.

Serve hot or cold with double cream, ice cream or on its own.

PINEAPPLE AND MANGO CRUMBLE

1 large	*mango, peeled and cut into pieces*
½ small	*fresh pineapple, peeled and cut into pieces*
100g (4 oz)	*plain flour*
40g (1½ oz)	*rolled oats*
75g (3 oz)	*brown sugar*
100g (4 oz)	*margarine*
½ tsp.	*cinnamon*
½ tsp.	*ginger powder*
½ tsp.	*nutmeg, grated*
½ tsp.	*vanilla*
25g (1 oz)	*granulated sugar*
1 tbsp.	*brown sugar to sprinkle on top*

1. Sift flour into a mixing bowl. Add cinnamon and ginger. Rub in margarine until mixture resembles breadcrumbs.
2. Stir in brown sugar and oats.
3. Mix together pineapple, mango, granulated sugar, vanilla and nutmeg. Put into a greased pie dish. Spoon over the crumble topping.
4. Sprinkle 1 tablespoon of brown sugar over crumble.
5. Bake in oven (375°F/gas mark 5) for 30 to 35 minutes or until browned.

Serves 6

Serve hot with custard, double cream or ice cream.

BOOZY PINEAPPLE

2 medium	fresh pineapples, peeled and cut into thick slices
4 tbsp.	rum (white or dark)
1 tsp.	root ginger grated
75ml (3 fl oz)	thick double cream
75g (3 oz)	butter
3 tbsp.	icing sugar
1 tsp.	mixed spice
	sprigs of mint to garnish (optional)

1. Put rum in a dish, add pineapple slices and marinate for 30 minutes. Turn pineapple over once during marinating.
2. Melt butter in a saucepan. Stir in icing sugar, cream and mixed spice.
3. Coat each pineapple slice in the butter mixture.
4. Place pineapple slices on a rack over hot coals or under a preheated grill. Barbecue or grill for 5 minutes each side or until golden brown.
5. Remove pineapple slices, sprinkle over grated ginger. Dust lightly with icing sugar and garnish with mint leaves.

Serve warm on its own, with vanilla ice cream, cream or drizzled with a sweet sauce of your choice

STEAMED MANGO AND ORANGE WITH RUM

1 large	firm ripe mango, peeled and cut into small pieces
2	oranges, peeled, deseeded and cut into segments
2 tbsp.	rum (white or dark)
1	cinnamon stick
3 tbsp.	light brown sugar
½ tsp.	root ginger, peeled and crushed.
¼ tsp.	nutmeg
¼ tsp.	vanilla
1	bay leaf

1. Put orange and mango into a greased oven proof dish. Add cinnamon stick and bay leaf.
2. Sprinkle over nutmeg, ginger and sugar. Add rum, vanilla and 2 tablespoons of cold water. Cover with baking foil.
3. Bake in a preheated oven (375°F/gas mark 5) for 20 minutes.
4. Remove cinnamon stick and bay leaf. Serve hot with ice cream, natural yoghurt or cream.

GRATER CAKE

2	fresh coconuts
900g (2lb)	granulated sugar
1 tsp.	root ginger, grated
	or ginger powder
	pink food colouring

1. Remove water and brown skin from flesh of coconut. Grate coconut finely.

2. Put sugar with ½ pint water in a thick bottom saucepan. Heat and stir until sugar dissolves.

3. Add coconut and ginger. Boil until coconut cooked to a thick sticky consistency that holds together.

4. Remove from heat and beat mixture for 2 to 3 minutes.

5. Spoon out 3 tablespoons of mixture and place in a dish. Add pink colouring.

6. Drop white mixture by spoonfuls into a greased tray, to make individual ones or pour into an 8-inch square dish and cut into squares when cooled.

7. Drop or spoon pink mixture on top of grater cakes.

Makes approx. 12

COCONUT DROPS

2	fresh coconuts, diced
900g (2lb)	brown sugar
1 tbsp.	root ginger, grated
	or ginger powder
1 tsp.	vanilla

1. Put coconut in a thick bottomed saucepan. Add enough water to cover coconut. Simmer for 1 hour or until coconut is tender.

2. Add sugar, ginger and vanilla. Boil for approx. 20 minutes or until mixture becomes very sticky. Test by dropping a small amount into cold water and if it forms a hard ball, it is ready.

3. Drop mixture by tablespoonfuls onto greaseproof paper. Leave to set.

Makes approx. 12 to 14 drops.

GIZZADAS

450g (1lb)	plain flour
1 tsp.	baking powder
450g (1 lb)	brown sugar
1 large	coconut, grated
75g (3 oz)	margarine
½ tsp.	ginger powder
½ tsp.	cinnamon
¼ tsp.	nutmeg, grated
1 tsp.	vanilla
	salt to taste
1 tbsp.	brown or granulated sugar for brushing gizzadas.

GRATER CAKE, COCONUT DROPS & GIZZADAS

1. For pastry, sift flour and salt into a large bowl. Rub in margarine.
2. Mix half amount of sugar with ½ pint of cold water. Stir until dissolved.
3. Add to flour and margarine to form a pastry.
4. Roll out pastry on a floured surface. Divide into twelve pieces, and roll each piece into a ball.
5. Roll each ball out to approximately ½ inch thickness, and then use a saucer to cut into circles.
6. For filling, put remaining sugar into a saucepan, add ½ pint water and boil into syrup.
7. Add coconut, nutmeg, vanilla, ginger and cinnamon. Stir well and remove from heat.
8. Brush the edges of each pastry circle with cold water.
9. Put one tablespoon of coconut mixture in one half of each circle.
10. Fold over other half of circle and press down with a fork.
11. Place gizzadas approx. 1 inch apart on a large greased baking tray.
12. Bake in a preheated oven (400°F/gas mark 6) for 15 to 20 minutes or until pastry is golden brown.
13. Make syrup of 1 tablespoon of sugar and warm water. Brush each gizzada with syrup as you remove them from oven.

TROPICAL PANCAKES

PANCAKE MIX

100g (4 oz)   plain flour
1   egg
300ml   milk
(½ Pint)

              pinch of salt
              oil for frying

*M*akes 8 thin pancakes.

1. Sift flour and salt into a bowl. Make a well in the centre and drop in egg. Fold in flour gradually.
2. Whisk in half of the milk to a thick batter. Put in fridge or cool place for at least 20 minutes.
3. Lightly grease an 8-inch frying pan.
4. Add remaining milk to batter mix. Stir well.
5. Pour in enough batter mix to coat the base of the frying pan.
6. Cook for 1 to 2 minutes until browned. Flip over and cook other side until browned.
7. Layer the pancakes on a plate.

FILLINGS
GUAVA

1   tin guava halves in syrup
½ tsp.   grated ginger or ginger powder
½ tsp.   cinnamon

1. Drain guavas
2. Sprinkle over cinnamon and ginger
3. Divide guavas between pancakes
4. Drizzle some of syrup over guavas.
5. Fold pancakes into quarters.

COCONUT

8 oz   fresh coconut grated
3 tbsp.   brown sugar
½ tsp.   mixed spice
           pinch saffron (optional)

1. Mix coconut, ginger, sugar and mixed spice
2. Spread a spoonful of mixture on pancake and fold into quarters
3. Decorate with saffron and with remaining coconut.

BANANA

4   firm ripe bananas, peeled and sliced
1 tsp.   grated ginger or ginger powder
2 oz   brown sugar
1 oz   butter
1   lemon

1. Mix ginger and sugar
2. Sprinkle lemon juice over bananas
3. Heat butter in a frying pan
4. Fry bananas until golden brown
5. Toss in sugar and ginger
6. Divide equally between pancakes and fold into quarters.

SPICED BANANAS

4	ripe bananas, peeled
4 tbsp.	brown sugar
1 tbsp.	lemon juice
1 tbsp.	lime juice
1 tsp.	mixed spice
2 oz.	butter

1. Place bananas in a greased ovenproof dish.
2. Sprinkle with lemon and lime juice. Sprinkle 1 tablespoon of sugar over each banana.
3. Cream butter with mixed spice and dot each banana.
4. Bake in a preheated oven (375°F/gas mark 5) for 15 to 20 minutes until cooked.
5. Serve hot or cold with cream or ice cream.

Serves 6

BAKED COCONUT BANANAS

6	under ripe bananas, unpeeled
3 tbsp.	grated fresh coconut or desiccated coconut
50g (2 oz)	brown sugar
1 tsp.	mixed spice
3 tsp.	orange juice

1. Mix together coconut, sugar and mixed spice.
2. Make a slit along the top surface of each banana.
3. Pour ½ teaspoon of orange juice in each slit.
4. Fill each slit with the coconut mixture.
5. Reshape the bananas and wrap each one tightly in baking foil.
6. Place directly on medium hot coals. Barbecue for 5 minutes on each side. Or in a preheated oven (400°F/gas mark 6).
7. To serve slightly open banana skins and serve with whipped cream or ice cream.

Serves 6

TROPICAL FRUIT SALAD

1	ripe pineapple
2	bananas, sliced
1	ripe honeydew melon
1	paw paw (papaya), deseeded and cut into slices
1	mango, peeled, stoned and cut into slices
1	tin guava halves in syrup
100g (4 oz)	grapes (black and green)
1 small	coconut, flesh diced. Cut some strips to decorate also.
2	kumquats, sliced
2	oranges, peeled
50g (2 oz)	root ginger, chopped
1	cinnamon stick
3 tsp.	dark rum (optional)
1	lime, juiced and peel grated
2 tbsp.	brown sugar
	sprigs of mint to decorate

1. Cut melon and pineapple into halves. Remove flesh and place in a large bowl. Put shells aside.
2. Remove guavas from syrup and chop.
3. Halve and pip grapes.
4. Segment the oranges over the bowl to catch the juice.
5. Put all the fruit into bowl with melon, orange and pineapple and sprinkle over lime juice.
6. Put half amount of guava syrup into a saucepan, add sugar, lime peel, cinnamon stick and ginger. Bring to the boil. Remove from heat and leave to cool. Remove cinnamon stick and strain syrup.
7. Pour cooled syrup over fruit, add rum and stir. Cover with cling film and chill for at least 1 hour.
8. Serve in bowls or pineapple and melon shells.
9. Decorate with mint and strips of coconut.

Serves 6 to 8

Serve with cream, ice cream or natural yoghurt.

You can omit or add fresh fruit of your choice.

BANANA ICE CREAM

3	*bananas, mashed*
2	*eggs*
75g (3oz)	*castor sugar*
300ml (½ Pint)	*milk*
300ml (½ Pint)	*double cream or evaporated milk*
1 tsp.	*vanilla*

1. Beat eggs and whisk in milk.
2. Strain into a thick-based saucepan, stirring all the time heat gently until mixture thickens.
3. Add sugar and vanilla essence. Leave to cool.
4. Whip the cream or evaporated milk until slightly thickened and fold into the mixture.
5. Stir in mashed bananas.
6. Pour into a container, cover and place in freezer until half frozen.
7. Remove and whisk thoroughly. Return to freezer until firm.

MANGO ICE CREAM

2	*ripe mangoes*
100g (4 oz)	*icing sugar*
300ml (½ pint)	*double cream*
2	*limes, juiced*

1. Peel mangoes, remove flesh and chop finely.
2. Put chopped mango with other ingredients in a blender or whisk thoroughly.
3. Put into a tub or container, cover and freeze for 2 hours.
4. Remove from freezer and whisk well, then return to freezer until firm.

MANGO SORBET

3 large	ripe mangoes, peeled and stoned
225g (8oz)	castor sugar
2	egg whites
600ml (1 pint)	water
	mint leaves to decorate (optional)

1. Put sugar and water in a saucepan. Heat gently until sugar dissolved. Bring to boil and simmer for 5 minutes. Remove from heat and leave syrup to cool completely.
2. Purée mangoes, and add to syrup.
3. Pour into a container and freeze until thick and slushy.
4. Whisk egg whites until stiff.
5. Remove mango mixture from freezer and mix until smooth.
6. Fold mango mixture into egg whites.
7. Return to freezer, and freeze until firm.
8. Remove from freezer approx. 10 minutes before serving. Spoon into sundae dishes or stemmed glasses and decorate with mint leaves.

RUM AND RAISIN ICE CREAM

100g (4 oz)	raisins
2 tbsp.	dark rum
300ml (½ pint)	condensed milk
300ml (½ pint)	evaporated milk
½ tsp.	vanilla

1. Mix condensed and evaporated milk.
2. Fold in raisins, vanilla and rum.
3. Pour into a container and place in freezer until half-frozen.
4. Remove and stir thoroughly. Return to freezer until firm.

COCONUT ICE CREAM

300ml (½ pint)	coconut milk
300ml (½ pint)	evaporated milk
300 ml (½ pint)	condensed milk
1 tsp.	vanilla
½ tsp.	nutmeg

1. Mix all the milks together. Stir in vanilla and nutmeg.
2. Pour into a container and place in freezer until half frozen.
3. Remove from freezer and whisk thoroughly.
4. Cover and return to freezer until firm.

FROZEN GUAVA CREAM

1	tin guavas, drained and chopped
100g (4 oz)	castor sugar
100g (4 oz)	natural yoghurt
8 fl oz	whipping cream
2	egg whites
1 tbsp.	lemon juice
	mint leaves to decorate (optional)

1. Beat together egg whites, sugar and lemon juice until fluffy and thick.
2. Whip cream and fold into egg white and sugar mixture. Add guava and yoghurt. Mix well.
3. Put mixture into a freezing tray or shallow container.
4. Cover and freeze for at least 4 hours or overnight.
5. Serve in small dishes or stemmed glasses and decorate with mint leaves.

BACK 'N' FRONT

1 large   *block of ice*
pineapple or strawberry syrup
vanilla ice cream

1. Shave or crush ice and put into tall glasses.
2. Pour over syrup.
3. Add 2 scoops of ice cream.
4. Repeat process until glasses are full.

Serve immediately

Back 'n' front and snowball were two of my childhood favourites. The equivalent to ice cream vendors used to travel around districts or visit the schools at lunchtime. They used little carts or vans, which contained ice cream, various syrups and huge blocks of ice packed in straw and muslin bags. They would use an ice shaver to shave the ice. Children would run with excitement to order these treats.

BACK 'N' FRONT

SNOW BALL

1 large   *block of ice*
pineapple or strawberry syrup
lime or lemon juice

1. Shave or crush ice and pack tightly into tumbler glasses.
2. Pour over syrup and limejuice.

Serve immediately

RUM AND CHOCOLATE SOUFFLES

2 tbsp.	dark rum
75g (3 oz)	plain chocolate, chopped
8 fl oz	double cream
4	eggs, separated
100g (4 oz)	icing sugar, sifted
½ tsp.	vanilla
	grated chocolate to decorate

1. Tie a double band of foil tightly around a soufflé dish or 6 ramekins. Make sure the foil stands 1 inch above rim.

2. Gently heat the chopped chocolate with 1 tablespoon of water in a saucepan. When melted cool slightly.

3. Whisk egg yolks and icing sugar until thick and creamy.

4. Whisk melted chocolate into egg and icing sugar mixture.

5. Whip cream, vanilla and rum until stiff. Fold into chocolate mixture.

6. Whisk egg whites until stiff. Gently fold into chocolate mixture.

7. Pour into ramekins or souffle dish and freeze for 4 hours or until firm.

8. Transfer to fridge 10 minutes before serving to soften.

9. Remove foil and sprinkle grated chocolate over top.

Serves 4 to 6

TAMARIND BALLS

900g (2 lb)	tamarinds or tamarind block
900g (2 lb)	brown sugar
	granulated sugar for coating

1. If using fresh tamarinds, remove shells from tamarinds. Remove flesh from seeds.

   If using a tamarind block, cut into small pieces.

2. Mix tamarind flesh with brown sugar. Knead and roll into small balls.

3. Roll the balls in granulated sugar.

4. Store in airtight jars.

Makes approx. 40 – 50 balls.

SEASONINGS, SAUCES, DIPS & OILS

JERK SEASONING

Jerk seasoning is very hot and spicy. It is used for Jamaica's famous jerk chicken and pork. It is usually used as a marinade for poultry, meat and fish. It can be used sparingly to add flavour and hotness to most dishes. The dry jerk seasoning can be added to flour and breadcrumbs as a coating.

Whilst jerk seasoning can be rubbed into meat or fish and cooked immediately, for best results leave for at least 2 hours, preferably overnight – You will not regret the wait!

WET SEASONING

4 stalks	escallion or spring onion, chopped
6	scotch bonnet peppers (mixed colours) chopped with seeds
3 cloves	garlic, chopped
1 large	onion, chopped
1 sprig	thyme
1 sprig	rosemary
2 tbsp.	vegetable oil
1 tbsp.	vinegar
1 tsp.	salt
2 tbsp.	lime juice
1 tsp.	pimento seeds

1. Wash and thoroughly dry a jar or airtight container (approx. 1lb).
2. Put all ingredients in a blender, or mash into a thick paste.
3. Put seasoning in jar or container.

*L*asts for 3 to 4 weeks.

DRY SEASONING

4 stalks	escallion or spring onion dried and chopped finely
12	poinsettia (bird) peppers, dried
2 tbsp.	dried onion
1 tsp.	garlic powder
1 tsp.	ground ginger
1 tsp.	salt
2 tsp.	mixed herbs
1 tsp.	pimento seeds
1 tsp.	ground black pepper

1. Place all ingredients in a grinder and grind to a powder. Alternatively you can use a pestle and mortar or tie all the ingredients in a clean tea towel/ cloth and beat with a rolling pin.
2. Place seasoning in a clean jar or airtight container.

*L*asts up to 2 months.

SWEET AND TANGY MARINADE

150ml (¼ pint)	clear honey
3 tbsp.	soy sauce
3 tsp.	hot pepper sauce
150ml (¼ pint)	red wine vinegar
2 cloves	garlic, crushed
1	orange, grated peel and juice
1 tbsp.	lemon juice
½ tsp.	mixed herbs

1. Put all ingredients in a saucepan. Bring to the boil. Simmer until reduced to about a third in quantity.

2. Serve hot as a sauce or cool and use as a marinade or glaze for chicken and pork.

BARBECUE SAUCE

3 tbsp.	tomato ketchup
1 tsp.	chilli powder
2 tbsp.	soft brown sugar
1 tsp.	dry mustard
150ml (¼ pint)	vegetable stock
3	bay leaves
1 clove	garlic, crushed
2 tbsp.	vinegar
1 tsp.	salt

1. Mix all the ingredients in a saucepan.

2. Bring to the boil, then cover and simmer for 15 minutes or until thickened.

3. Remove bay leaves.

4. Serve hot as a sauce or leave to cool and use as a marinade.

*D*elicious as a sauce with fried chicken. Use as a marinade for spare ribs, other meats, poultry and fish.

FENNEL AND CITRUS MARINADE

4	limes, grated peel and juice
2	lemons, grated peel and juice
½ tsp.	root ginger, grated
2 tsp.	fennel seeds
6 tbsp.	vegetable oil
12	peppercorns, bruised
½ tsp.	salt

1. Mix all the ingredients together. Cover and leave overnight.

2. Strain marinade before using or place in an airtight jar or container.

*U*se as a marinade with a sharp bite for fish and seafood.

RUNDOWN SAUCE

20 fl oz (1 pint)	coconut milk
1 large	onion, finely chopped
1	hot pepper, deseeded and finely chopped
100g (4 oz)	sweet pepper, diced
1 tbsp.	vinegar
1	tomato, finely chopped
1 clove	garlic, crushed
2 stalks	escallion, finely chopped
4	pimento seeds or cloves
1 sprig	thyme
2	bay leaves
½ tsp.	ground black pepper
1	lime, juiced

1. Pour coconut milk into a saucepan and bring to the boil. Simmer for approximately 1 hour or until it starts to turn oily.
2. Add remaining ingredients and simmer for 10 minutes.
3. Serve immediately or leave to cool, spoon into a jar and store in the fridge.

*L*asts up to 1 week.

*S*erve with seafood, poultry or vegetable dishes. Can be added to flavour curries and stews.

*T*his sauce is usually served as above, however, as an option you can blend it until smooth.

GUAVA SAUCE

4 tbsp.	guava jelly
½ tsp.	dried mixed herbs
½ tsp.	root ginger, finely chopped
1 clove	garlic, finely chopped
1 tbsp.	oil
50ml (2 fl oz)	white wine vinegar
75ml (3 fl oz)	orange juice
	salt to taste

1. Warm orange juice in a saucepan. Add guava jelly and stir until melted.
2. Add all remaining ingredients. Stir and simmer for 2 minutes.
3. Serve immediately with meat, fish, poultry or over salad.

JAMAICAN PICKLED PEPPER

This is a favourite pickle in Jamaica, used on a daily basis. With its very hot flavour, it is advisable to use very sparingly.

12	*scotch bonnet peppers, a selection of colours.*
½	*chocho, peeled and diced*
1	*carrot, peeled and diced*
¼	*cucumber, peeled and diced*
1	*onion, halved and thinly sliced*
6	*peppercorns*
4	*pimento seeds or cloves*
1	*pint white vinegar*
2 tsp.	*salt*

1. Using a knife and fork cut open the scotch bonnet peppers. Remove seeds and core. Coarsely chop and put into a large bowl of cold water with salt.
2. Add remaining vegetables, cover and leave overnight.
3. Remove from water and drain thoroughly.
4. Pack into jars and cover with vinegar.
5. Leave for at least one week before using.

*L*asts for 2 to 3 months.

*S*erve with jerk pork/chicken, barbecued meats and fried fish.

PICKLED PEPPER, TAMARIND CHUTNEY, MANGO CHUTNEY

TAMARIND CHUTNEY

100g (4 oz)	seedless tamarind
6 fl oz	water
3 tbsp.	sugar
½ tsp.	salt
1 tsp.	cumin powder, roasted
½ tsp.	chilli powder
½ tsp.	nutmeg
½ medium	onion, grated
½ tsp.	balsamic vinegar
	pinch dried tarragon

1. Put tamarind and water in a saucepan, and bring to the boil. Simmer for a few minutes until tamarind has melted.
2. Add all the other ingredients and stir well. Leave to cool.
3. Liquidize mixture and put into an airtight jar or container.

*L*asts for approximately 1 month.

*S*erve with meat, fish or vegetable dishes.

MANGO CHUTNEY

1 large	mango, under ripe
3 tbsp.	raisins
1 small	onion, finely chopped
¼ tsp.	ginger powder
100g (4 oz)	brown sugar
½ tsp.	mixed spice
¼ tsp.	scotch bonnet pepper, finely chopped
1 tbsp.	vinegar
¼ tsp.	salt

1. Peel the mango and cut flesh into pieces.
2. Place all the ingredients in a large heavy saucepan. Add enough water to cover.
3. Bring to the boil and simmer for approximately 30 minutes stirring occasionally. Water should boil down until the mixture reaches a thick consistency.
4. Cool and put into jars.

*L*asts for 3 to 4 weeks.

*S*erve with curries and cold meat dishes.

CHILLI DIP

3	red chillies, chopped
3	ripe tomatoes, quartered
1 clove	garlic, crushed
4 sprigs	parsley, chopped

1. Put all ingredients in a liquidizer until smooth but lumpy consistency.
2. Serve immediately or put in a container and store in the fridge.

Delicious with most dishes.

YOGHURT AND HERB DIP

7 fl oz	natural yoghurt
½ tsp.	fresh basil, finely chopped
½ tsp.	chives, chopped
½ tsp.	fresh mint, chopped
2 spring	onions, finely chopped
1 clove	garlic, crushed
¼ tsp.	paprika
1 tbsp.	lemon juice
	salt and pepper to taste
	sprigs of mint to garnish

1. Mix yoghurt and lemon juice in a large bowl. Season with salt and pepper.
2. Stir in rest of the ingredients.
3. Spoon into a serving dish and chill. Garnish with sprigs of mint when ready to serve.

Serve with savoury biscuits, pitta bread or raw vegetables such as red and green peppers, celery, carrot etc.

CHILLI DIP, YOGHURT & HERB DIP, PINEAPPLE SALSA AND TOMATO SAUCE

PINEAPPLE SALSA

1 small	ripe pineapple, peeled and chopped or 1 small tin of pineapple drained and chopped.
1 clove	garlic, crushed
2 stalks	escallion or spring onions, chopped
25g (1 oz)	root ginger, peeled and chopped
1 tsp.	brown sugar
2 tsp.	hot pepper sauce
1 tbsp.	vegetable oil
½ tsp.	fresh rosemary, finely chopped

1. Put all ingredients in a bowl. Mix well
2. Serve chilled.

Serve with jerk chicken, jerk pork, barbecued meats and fish.

Tip
Try using mango instead of pineapple as a variation.

TOMATO SAUCE

900g (2 lb)	ripe tomatoes, cut up into pieces
1 medium	onion, finely chopped
1 clove	garlic, crushed
2 tbsp.	oil
1 tsp.	salt
50g (2 oz)	sugar
6 fl oz	vinegar
1	bouquet garni - e.g. thyme, peppercorns, parsley, mixed herbs, bay leaf, clove
½ tsp.	paprika
	pinch cayenne pepper

1. Heat oil in a saucepan. Fry onion until beginning to soften. Add garlic and tomatoes. Simmer gently until tomatoes pulped.
2. Put through a sieve or mash with a potato masher or wooden spoon.
3. Pour mixture back into the pan and add remaining ingredients.
4. Bring to the boil. Simmer until a creamy consistency, stirring occasionally.
5. Remove bouquet garni. Serve immediately or cool and pour into jars/bottles.

MAYONNAISE

2 tsp.	*white wine vinegar or lemon juice*
1	*egg yolk*
½ tsp.	*mustard*
5 fl oz	*olive oil or corn oil*
	pinch of salt

1. Whisk together mustard, egg yolk and salt in a bowl.
2. While whisking add oil drop by drop. Increase to a steady stream as mixture thickens.
3. Steadily beat in vinegar or lemon juice. If too thick beat in a little hot water.

Variations: Herb mayonnaise - add 2 tablespoons of fresh chopped herbs such as chives, tarragon, parsley or mixed herbs.
Garlic mayonnaise – grind 2 cloves of garlic and add to the egg yolk.

VINAIGRETTE DRESSING

6 tsp.	*white wine vinegar*
3 fl oz	*olive or corn oil*
1 tbsp.	*lemon juice*
½ tsp.	*mustard*
	pinch salt
	pinch freshly ground black pepper

1. Place all ingredients in a screw – top jar and shake vigorously until well blended.

Serve as a dressing – ideal dressing for salads.

Variations: Herb dressing – add 1 to 2 tablespoons of chopped fresh herbs such as basil, chives, parsley, or mixed herbs.
Garlic dressing – add 1 to 2 crushed cloves of garlic.

COCONUT MILK

2   dried coconuts
150ml   boiling water
(¼ pint)

1. Pierce the eyes of the coconuts and drain out the water into a jug.
2. Crack the shells with a hammer. Remove the flesh with a knife.
3. Grate the coconuts finely or cut into pieces and put in a blender.
4. Put grated coconut in a bowl. Pour over coconut water and ¼ pint of boiling water. Leave to stand for one hour.
5. Squeeze through a damp cloth.

For best results and freshness, use within 24 hours.

COCONUT CREAM

Leave the coconut milk to stand until the cream rises to the top. Skim off the cream and use as required.

Can be used for a coconut cream dessert.

COCONUT OIL

2   dried coconuts
150ml   water
(¼ pint)

1. Grate or blend coconuts as above.
2. Add ¼ pint of water to coconut. Knead mixture for about 5 minutes. Squeeze through a cloth over a bowl to remove milk.
3. Put coconut milk in a saucepan. Bring to the boil, then simmer for 1 to 1½ hours until it turns to oil.
4. Strain and leave to cool.
5. Pour oil into a clean bottle and use as required. Will last 2 to 3 weeks.

FLAVOURED OILS
ANNATTO IN COCONUT OIL

2 tbsp.   annatto seeds
600ml   coconut oil
(1 pint)

1. Put annatto seeds into a clean bottle.
2. Pour over oil. Leave for a week to allow oil to become orangey/red in colour.
3. Shake bottle and allow seeds to settle, before use. Seeds are not usually used.

L asts for up to 1 month

U se for shallow frying/browning and marinades. Use for adding colour and flavour to fish, chicken and stews.
Adds colour to rice and saltfish fritters.

T ip If you can't get annatto seeds try using ½ teaspoon of saffron.

TARRAGON IN OLIVE OIL

4 sprigs   fresh tarragon
600ml (1 pint) extra virgin olive oil

1. Wash and pat dry the tarragon.
2. Put tarragon in a clean bottle and fill with the olive oil, making sure the tarragon is covered.
3. Store in a cool dry place.
4. For a rich aromatic flavour, leave for a week before using.

L asts 3 to 4 weeks.

U se sparingly for shallow frying and marinades. Can be used for meat and fish.

HERB OIL

2 sprigs	thyme
2 sprigs	rosemary
4 cloves	garlic
12	peppercorns
600ml (1 pint)	sunflower oil

1. Wash and dry thyme, rosemary and garlic. Put into a clean bottle with the peppercorns.
2. Add sunflower oil, covering the herbs.
3. Store in a cool dry place.
4. Leave for about 3 to 4 days before using.

*L*asts 3 to 5 weeks.

GINGER IN VEGETABLE OIL

100g (4 oz)	piece of root ginger
600ml (1 pint)	vegetable oil

1. Peel ginger and cut into strips or slices. Put into a clean bottle.
2. Fill bottle with oil to cover all of the ginger.
3. Store in a cool dry place.

*L*asts 4 to 6 weeks.

*U*se for frying and marinades for meat, fish and vegetables.

CITRUS OIL

6	limes or lemons
600ml	sunflower oil
(1 pint)	

1. Wash and dry limes or lemons. Slice thinly. Put into a wide rimmed airtight jar.
2. Pour over oil to cover limes or lemons.
3. Leave to marinate for 1 week.

*L*asts approximately 2 weeks.

*U*se for frying, marinades and oil dressing for salads. use for fish, meat and vegetables.

SWEET PEPPERS IN TARRAGON VINEGAR

3	sweet peppers, red/yellow/green
300ml (½ pint)	vinegar
3 Sprigs	fresh tarragon

1. Wash and dry peppers. Remove core and deseed. Cut peppers into large strips.
2. Put peppers and tarragon in a wide neck jar.
3. Fill with the vinegar.
4. Store in a cool dry place for a week before using.

*S*erve peppers as a side dish with hot or cold meats, or in salads. Vinegar can be used for flavouring and marinades.

DRINKS

CARROT PUNCH

675g (1 ½ lb)	carrots
1 bottle/tin	stout or guinness
1 tin	vanilla nutriment
1 pint	fresh milk
½ tin	condensed milk
½ tsp.	nutmeg
½ tsp.	vanilla

1. Peel and grate carrots. Put into a muslin cloth or clean tea towel and squeeze out juice into a large jug.
2. Add all other ingredients into jug and mix well.
3. Cover with cling film and chill in fridge.

Add ice cubes just before serving.

Serves 6

For an even richer taste add a generous amount of vanilla ice cream. Rum can also be added if desired.

This punch is a must, served with traditional Sunday dinner mainly of rice & peas with chicken or curried goat.

CARROT PUNCH & SORREL

SORREL

225g (½ lb)	*sorrel*
25g (1 oz)	*root ginger*
3	*cloves*
3	*pimento seeds*
1	*cinnamon stick*
350g (12oz)	*sugar*
	(more for desired sweetness)
1	*lime, juiced*

1. Put sorrel, ginger, cloves, pimento and cinnamon into a large saucepan with lid.

2. Cover with 3 pints of water and bring to the boil. Simmer for 5 minutes. Remove from heat and leave for at least 4 hours preferably overnight.

3. Strain into a large jug and sweeten to taste with the sugar. Add lime juice.

4. Store in jug or bottles in the fridge.

5. Serve with ice.

For an extra kick add rum if desired.

This tangy and spicy drink is very popular in Jamaica at Christmas time.

CITRUS COOLER

1	*measure of dark rum*
2 tbsp	*pineapple juice*
50ml / 2 fl oz	*dry white wine*
1½ tsp.	*castor sugar*
	lemonade or soda water to top up

1. Shake all the ingredients with ice.
2. Strain into a tall glass and top up with lemonade or soda.
3. Decorate with pineapple or lemon slices.

PINEAPPLE FIZZ SPECIAL

4 fl oz	*sparkling white wine, chilled*
3 fl oz	*pineapple juice, chilled*
1 tbsp	*lime juice*
1 tsp	*sugar*
	chopped mint to garnish

1. Put lime juice and sugar into a tall glass.
2. Pour over wine and pineapple juice.
3. Stir and garnish with chopped mint.

GINGER BEER

225g (8oz)   root ginger
2   cinnamon sticks
2   limes, juiced
675g   soft brown sugar
(1½lb)

1. Wash and beat ginger. Put ginger and cinnamon stick into a large saucepan with 5 pints of water. Bring to the boil and simmer for 10 minutes. Remove from heat and leave overnight.
2. Strain into a large jug or container.
3. Stir in sugar and lime juice. Add more sugar if not sweet enough or more water if too sweet.
4. Pour into bottles and chill.
5. Serve with ice.

FRUIT PUNCH

300ml (½ pint)   mango juice
300ml (½ pint)   pineapple juice
300ml (½ pint)   orange juice
300ml (½ pint)   guava juice
1   lemon, juiced
1   lime, juiced

1. Mix ingredients together. Chill in fridge in a large jug or bottles.
2. Serve with ice and pieces of fruit (optional).

SOURSOP PUNCH

1 large	ripe soursop or
35 fl oz	soursop juice
(1¾ pints)	
¼ tsp.	nutmeg
½ tsp.	vanilla
	condensed milk to taste

1. If using fresh soursop, scoop out pulp and remove core and seeds. Put pulp into a bowl and crush. Stir in 35 fl.oz (1¾ pint) of water and strain.
2. Add nutmeg, vanilla and condensed milk to the soursop juice.
3. Chill in the fridge. Serve with ice.

Serves 4

BANANA MILK SHAKE

4	ripe bananas
1200ml (2 pints)	cold milk
2	scoops vanilla ice cream
1 tsp.	vanilla

1. Peel and chop bananas.
2. Put all ingredients in a blender. Blend well.
3. Serve with ice in tall glasses.

Serves 4

RUM WITH COCONUT WATER

This refreshing drink is very popular in Jamaica. Rum is part of everyday life on the Island. This is one of the simpler, yet still exotic and satisfying ways it is served.

1   *fresh green coconut*
1   *generous measure of white or dark rum*
     sugar to taste

1. Slice the top off the coconut.
2. Pour rum and sugar (if desired) into coconut.
3. Shake and serve with a straw.
4. Add crushed ice if desired.

Once you have enjoyed your drink, spoon out and eat the jelly for an added treat.

Alternatively mix coconut water, rum and sugar. Pour into a tumbler over crushed ice.

RUM PUNCH

1   *measure sour (lime juice)*
2   *measures of sweet (sugar or syrup)*
3   *measures strong rum*
4   *measures of water or crushed ice*

1. Mix all ingredients together.
2. Garnish with slices of fruit such as orange and pineapple
3. Serve in punch glasses.

Fruit juice such as pineapple or orange can be added if desired

DAIQUIRI

2	measures dark rum
1 tsp.	castor sugar
1 tbsp	lime or lemon juice

1. Blend all ingredients well
2. Serve over crushed ice and decorate with a cherry

Variations: Add ½ ripe banana and blend until smooth and frothy. Try adding pineapple juice and cointreau for a pineapple daiquiri. Or try mango finely chopped with curacao, blended to a slushy consistency for mango daiquiri.

RUM CREAM

2	measures strong rum
1	measure double cream
1 tsp	sugar

1. Shake the ingredients vigorously with cracked ice.
2. Strain into a cocktail glass.

SANTA CRUZ

1	measure dark rum
½	measure cherry brandy
1 tsp	sugar
1 tsp	water
	juice of ½ lemon

1. Put sugar and water in a tall glass
2. Dissolve sugar and add remaining ingredients.
3. Fill with crushed ice and stir slowly.
4. Add a slice of lemon and serve.

JAMAICAN COFFEE

white rum
strong black Blue Mountain coffee
or strong coffee of your choice.
double cream
soft brown sugar

1. Put 1 tablespoon rum in a warmed coffee or heatproof glass.
2. Pour over strong black Blue Mountain coffee within ½ inch of the top.
3. Add sugar to taste.
4. Pour over a thick layer of cream.

MALIBU MOCHA

2 tbsp   malibu
2 tsp   drinking chocolate
½ tsp   coffee granules
2tbsp   single cream
*   grated chocolate and whipped*
*   cream to decorate*
*   boiling water*

1. Pour water into a heatproof glass.
2. Stir in coffee and drinking chocolate
3. Stir in cream and Malibu.
4. Serve with a spoonful of whipped cream and sprinkling of grated chocolate.

WARM GINGER AND RUM PUNCH

2 tsp   rum
4 fl oz   ginger wine
3 tbsp   orange juice
1   cinnamon stick
*   orange slices (optional)*

1. Put all ingredients in a saucepan and warm gently.
2. Strain into a heatproof glass.
3. Garnish with orange slices and serve.

MINT TEA

2 sprigs mint
Sugar to taste

1. Put mint with ½ pint of cold water in a saucepan.
2. Bring to the boil and simmer for 2 to 3 minutes.
3. Strain into a cup and add sugar to taste.

GINGER TEA

25g (1 oz) Root ginger
Sugar to taste

1. Beat ginger.
2. Put into a saucepan with ½ pint cold water.
3. Bring to boil. Lower heat and simmer for 2 to 3 minutes.
4. Strain into a cup and add sugar to taste.

LEMON/LIME TEA

Dried lemon or lime peel
Sugar to taste

1. Put dried peel in a saucepan with ½ pint water.
2. Bring to the boil and simmer for a couple of minutes.
3. Strain into a cup and add sugar to taste.
4. Serve with slices of lemon or lime.

Condensed milk or honey can be added instead of sugar to all the above teas.

HERBS AND SPICES

Herbs and spices are part of every day cooking in the Caribbean. They are used to enhance and improve the taste of dishes. They are what help to create tasty, spicy food, which is one of the trademarks of Jamaica. Obviously fresh herbs are best, and some are not that difficult to grow, such as thyme, basil, rosemary, mint, sage etc. You do not need to have a great deal of space, as most herbs will grow in pots and window boxes. There is nothing better than adding your own freshly grown herbs to your cooking.

Dried herbs are a good substitute, but obviously not as good. Dried herbs are more concentrated and stronger in flavour; therefore you need smaller amounts. Spices have such distinctive colours and flavours making food more appetising. Hot and aromatic spices can help to create exotic dishes, whilst transforming bland everyday ingredients.

Herbs and spices will help you create the special blend of heat and fragrance in your cooking. In indulging in Caribbean cooking you will be embarking on an exotic journey of taste and aroma. Part of this journey will involve experiencing the benefits and pleasures of herbs and spices.

Our jerk seasoning is a typical example of how herbs and spices have been combined over centuries to create a unique hot spicy flavour for poultry, meat and fish. Jerk cooking has been part of culinary tradition in Jamaica, referring to a highly seasoned spiced dish cooked slowly in a fire pit on pimento wood.

Once you have started experimenting with herbs and spices, there is no end to the range of flavours you can create. The list below contains herbs and spices used in the recipes; however, it also contains others that you may want to try.

Storing Herbs

If you buy dried herbs, you should keep them in the containers which they come in.

Drying your own:

You should dry herbs just before they begin to flower. Dry them soon after picking. Loosely tie them in a bundle and hang them upside down in a cool dry place for several weeks. When the leaves are dried, rub them off and store in airtight jars, away from direct light.

They can also be placed in a slow oven to dry. A quicker method is to put sprigs of herbs between kitchen towels and place them in the microwave on high power until the leaves become brittle.

Fresh herbs:
Herbs with long stalks can be put in a jug of water and left at room temperature, or covered with a plastic bag and placed in the fridge. Herbs can be kept in the fridge for up to a week. Those with short stalks can be placed in a plastic bag. Some herbs such as basil, mint, tarragon, parsley and dill freeze very well and will keep for about six months. Rinse the herbs and pat dry, then place them in plastic freezer bags and press out any air. Use them from the freezer as required. Alternatively you can freeze them in small blocks in ice trays and use as required.

Cooking with fresh herbs
The recipe and the herb itself will usually determine how it is used in cooking. Whole leaves or sprigs can be added to salads or used as a garnish e.g. basil, chive and parsley. Chopped raw herbs can be used in cold sauces, marinades, dips and salsa e.g. mint, garlic, chives. Herbs such as basil, annatto and rosemary add flavour to oils for frying and marinating. Speciality vinegars are infused with herbs and spices such as tarragon, garlic, ginger, peppercorns, pimento, chilli etc. These oils and vinegars not only look colourful but also add aromatic flavour to food in cooking itself. Some herbs have soft leaves, so in order to prevent them losing their flavour they are added towards the end of cooking e.g. basil and tarragon. Some herbs are hardier and benefit from lengthy cooking. These include rosemary and thyme, which are usually added with their stalks and removed before serving. In Jamaica seasoning, marinating and cooking with herbs and spices is compulsory . . . bland food is definitely a no no.

Bouquet Garni
Ready prepared bouquet garni in sachets, made from dried herbs can be bought. However, it is more fun and beneficial to make your own. Bouquet garni are usually herbs tied together in cotton or muslin, and used in soups, stews, sauces stocks etc. They are removed before serving. Your usual bouquet garni contains herbs such as parsley, chervil, marjoram, thyme and bay leaf. However, in Jamaica they are usually made with: escallion, thyme, pimento, peppercorns, bayleaf and hot pepper. They are made up or can be bought in bundles.

Depending on the recipe and herbs you have available, you can create your own with fresh or dried herbs.

Mixed herbs
This is usually a combination of dried herbs such as parsley, tarragon, thyme, chives and chervil. You can buy this ready made up. However, you can also make up your own.

ANNATTO: The seeds of a small flowering tree. Native to West Indies and tropical America. Orangey/red to seeds are used as flavouring and add colour to soups, fish and meat dishes.

BASIL: Fragrant aromatic herb with tender green leaves used worldwide. Compliments savoury dishes, meats, soups and salads. Adds flavour to marinades and sauces.

BAY LEAVES: Used for pickling, flavouring soups, stews and casseroles. Excellent in meat and seafood cooking. An essential ingredient for bouquet garni.

CAYENNE PEPPER: A spicy pungent powder made from red chillies. Should be used sparingly to flavour meat, fish, vegetables and sauces.

CELERY: Ground aromatic seeds of a plant related to the vegetable celery. Used in stews, meat, fish and salad dishes. Also used as a pickling spice.

CHILLI PEPPER: Little peppers grown on a dwarf bush. Peppers are red or green. The red is hotter and fiery. Used in meat, fish and soups. Chilli powder is usually used as a seasoning.

CHIVES: A flavour similar to escallion and onion. The grass like leaves are used in meat dishes, soups, salads and raw vegetables. Best used when freshly cut.

CINNAMON: Available in bark (rolled into sticks) or ground powdered form. Pungent sweet spice used for baking, puddings, sweets and pickling.

CLOVES: Nail shaped flower bud with a pungent aroma. Available whole or ground. Used for pickling, seasonings, and deserts, to stud ham or pork.

CURRY POWDER: Mixture of various spices. Used to flavour sauces, meat, fish and vegetable dishes.

DILL: Weed and seed form from the same plant. Mild slightly sweet flavour. Used in pickles, fish dishes and marinades.

ESCALLION: Part of onion family, resembling a spring onion, but with a stronger flavour. Very popular seasoning in Jamaica, used in most meat, fish and vegetable dishes.

FENNEL: Used as a herb and for its aromatic seeds. The bulb is used as a vegetable. Distinctive aniseed flavour, used with fish, in sauces and marinades.

GARLIC: Bulb of a plant belonging to the onion family. Used in segments known as cloves, powdered and salt. Widely used for meat, fish and vegetable dishes. Used in seasonings, marinades and sauces.

GINGER: From Jamaica, West Africa and Asia. Available in root, cracked and powder form.

Used in meat, fish and vegetable dishes, baking, sweets and beverages. Very good made as a tea for upset stomach. Also good for travel sickness.

HOT PEPPERS: The most pungent of all spices and should be used sparingly. Includes cayenne, red pepper, small hot chillies, scotch bonnet pepper etc. Adds hot intense flavour to dishes.

MACE: Fragrant dried covering around a nutmeg. In whole or ground form. Ground used for baking and in sauces. Whole used in pickling.

MARJORAM: Herb of the mint family. A delicate, sweet flavour with a slightly bitter undertone. Delicious in stews, soups, stocks and sauces. Can replace basil in meat dishes.

MINT: One of the most widely used herbs. With a fresh, strong, flavour and a cool after taste. Many varieties of mint. Mainly used in food for flavouring, garnishing, and drinks. Very easy to grow.

MUSTARD SEED: Three kinds. Black and brown contains the oil that gives a piquant flavour. White seeds have less flavour. Flavours meat, sauces and gravies. Used in pickles, relishes and chutney.

NUTMEG: Seed of the nutmeg tree. Sweet delicate flavour. Ground or whole. Grown extensively in the Caribbean. Used to flavour puddings, drinks, sauces and vegetables.

ONION: Belonging to same family as garlic. One of the most versatile seasonings. Used in a lot of meat, fish and vegetable dishes, sauces, marinades, chutneys, dips etc.

OREGANO: Also known as wild marjoram. Strong smelling herb with a trace of bitterness. Used in pasta, mince and tomato dishes. Good in salads and salad dressing.

PAPRIKA: Bright red powder made from dried sweet chilli pepper pods. Two varieties with sweet mild flavour or with a slight bite. Adds colour and flavour to vegetable dishes, seafood, poultry, soups and stews. A seasoning powder.

PARSLEY: One of best known and extensively used herbs. Various varieties. Mild flavour used as seasoning and garnish for soups, salads, meats, fish, sauces and vegetables.

PEPPER BLACK: Universally used spice. Whole or ground. Whole used for grinders. Used in meat, soups, bouquet garni and pickles. Ground adds flavour to most foods.

PEPPER WHITE: Whole or ground. Has a milder flavour than black pepper.

PIMENTO SEEDS: Also known as all spice. Flavour and aroma of a blend of spices, mainly nutmeg, cloves and cinnamon.

Used in sweet and savoury dishes, soups, pickles, seasonings, marinades and drinks. The wood and leaves of the tree used in Jamaica in jerk cooking.

POPPY SEEDS: Fragrant seeds of a type of poppy. Sprinkled on bread and cakes as decoration.

ROSEMARY: Pungent aromatic herb. Used for flavouring lamb, other meat, soups and stews. Also used in some sweet dishes, marinades and sauces.

SAGE: Slightly bitter herb. Popular for stuffings, pork, stews, hamburgers and salads.

Goes well in cheese as a spread.

SAFFRON: One of the most expensive spices from the flower stigmas of a type of crocus. Slightly bitter taste. Used for flavouring and colouring. Good in fish, chicken and soup dishes.

SCOTCH BONNET PEPPER: A very hot pepper, popular in Jamaican dishes. Used in soups, curried goat and chicken, seasonings and dishes needing an extra hot bite.

TARRAGON: Strong aromatic flavoured herb. Compatible with most foods. Used in sauces, fish, poultry, meat stews and vegetables. Makes very nice tarragon vinegar.

THYME: A strong pungent herb. Various varieties. Used in a lot of Caribbean dishes. Adds taste to roasts soups, meats, stews, fish, egg and tomato dishes.

TURMERIC: A bright orange/yellow powder with aromatic and slightly bitter flavour. Dried and ground roots of a plant of the ginger family. Essential ingredient of curry powder. Used for colouring and flavouring. Used in curries, fish and seafood, rice and meat dishes. Sometimes used as a substitute for saffron.

ACKEE: An edible fruit grown on an evergreen tree, introduced in the 18th century by West African slaves. The fruit has a scarlet shell, which encloses the yellow edible flesh. Inside the flesh are glossy black seeds. It is the flesh that is cooked, resembling scrambled eggs. It is served mainly as a traditional dish with salt fish.

ANNATTO: The seeds of a small flowering tree native to the West Indies and tropical America. Orangey/red in colour they are mainly used to flavour and colour food. They are also ground and used as a spice, or the whole seeds put in oil. It is also used as a substitute for turmeric or saffron.

AVOCADO PEAR: A pear shaped fruit with a rough green or black skin. It has a large brown stone encased in yellow flesh. They are eaten when ripe, with the stone being discarded. Avocados are popular in salads and as starters. In Jamaica they are served with bun and bulla cakes, and as an accompaniment with certain meals.

BAMMY: round flat bread made from grated cassava. Served with meat, fish or vegetable dishes. They are made quite thin or thick. They can also be toasted or fried after being soaked in milk or water.

BANANAS: Used a great deal in Caribbean cooking in their ripe and unripened state. In their unripened state are boiled and eaten as a vegetable. They are ripe when they have turned yellow, and are eaten as a fruit.

BREADFRUIT: A large round green skinned vegetable with a yellowish - white flesh, grown on a large leafy tree. Introduced by Captain Bligh. Breadfruits are only edible when cooked. Usually boiled or roasted and served as a vegetable, or added to soups and stews. They make a delicious snack made into chips.

BULLA CAKES: A popular round flat cake eaten on its own or with avocado pear or cheese.

CALLALOO: A vegetable leaf similar to spinach, rich in iron and vitamin C. An essential ingredient in Jamaica's pepperpot soup.

CASSAVA: A tropical vegetable with a long tuberous root, covered with a brown bark-like skin. The flesh inside is white and hard. It can be boiled and eaten as a vegetable. It is used for bammies, cakes, dumplings, flour etc. There are two types of cassava, bitter and sweet. The bitter one is poisonous until cooked. The sweet is eaten like a vegetable, whilst the bitter is grated and the juice removed before use.

CHOCHO: A light green or white pear shaped vegetable, which grows on a vine. It is similar to squash, but with a crisper and finer texture. It can be enjoyed boiled or steamed as a vegetable or cooked in soups, stews, meat and fish dishes. The flesh is sometimes used in pickles. It is sometimes blended with sugar for a sauce or pie.

COCO: A starchy root vegetable with a rough brown skin. It can be boiled as a vegetable or used to flavour soups and stews.

COCOA: The seed of the cocoa tree used to make chocolate.

COCONUT: Widely used fruit in Jamaica, for its water, milk, flesh and jelly. The shell and fibrous parts of the husk are used in making mats, mattresses, and craft products and in soil for plants. The flesh is also used to make soap and other body care products.

The water is some times drunk directly from a ripe coconut, or added to rum or fruit juices. The soft jelly inside the shell of a young coconut is a delicious delicacy. After the water has been drunk, the shell is split open and the jelly scooped out and eaten. The dry hard flesh of the older coconut nut is used in a variety of ways e.g. for coconut milk, cream and oil, sauces, puddings, cakes, sweets etc.

COFFEE: Jamaica produces one of the finest coffees in the world. Grown in the Blue Mountains, it has a rich full flavour.

DASHEEN: A round tuber vegetable with a hairy brown skin, and white hard flesh. It is peeled, boiled or roasted like a vegetable or put into soups and stews. It is similar to coco.

DUMPLINGS: Made with plain flour and boiled in water, dumplings are flat and round in shape. Small ones are added to soups and stews, whilst large ones are made to serve as an accompaniment to meat, fish and some vegetable dishes. Other ingredients such as cornmeal, grated green banana or cassava are added for different variations. The mixture can be made into other sizes and shapes known as spinners or drop spoon dumplings.

ESCALLION: Belonging to the onion family, the escallion looks similar to the spring onion, but has a stronger flavour. It is used as a seasoning in most savoury dishes in Jamaica.

GOAT, CURRY: One of Jamaica's most popular and traditional dishes. Goat flesh referred to as mutton is used, as there are not a lot of sheep in Jamaica. The meat is cut into cubes or pieces and highly seasoned with herbs and spices.

GUAVA: A greenish-yellow skinned fruit with a sweet pink or white flesh and a lot of seeds. It has a strong perfumed aroma.
Guavas are eaten raw, used in drinks, puddings, jellies and jams.

GUNGO PEAS: Also known as pigeon peas, are harvested in December. They are used in dried and fresh form known as green Gungo. The green is more popular being fresh and is used in rice & peas, soups and stews.

JERK: This type of cooking has become part of Jamaica's culinary tradition. It refers to a highly seasoned dish cooked slowly in a fire pit on pimento wood. Jerk seasoning is very hot and spicy highlighting Jamaica's famous jerk chicken and pork.

JOHNNY CAKE (Fried dumpling): A dough mixture fried in hot oil. Served as a snack, or with meat, fish or vegetable dishes. Usually served instead of rice, bread or boiled vegetables.

MANGO: A fleshy exotic fruit available in different sizes and varieties such as: Robin, Tommy Atkins and Bombay. Mangoes grow in abundance in Jamaica. They are green when unripe, then vary in colour when ripe, from green to deep red. The flesh inside which surrounds a large stone can be a light yellow colour to a deep orange. The ripe mango is eaten by itself, in fruit salads, drinks, ice creams, puddings and desserts. The unripe ones make good relishes and chutney.

MANNISH WATER: traditional highly seasoned soup made with goat meat and offal, and a wide variety of vegetables. Traditionally made in very large quantities to serve at social events such as weddings and festivals. It is believed to be an aphrodisiac for men.

OKRA (Ladies Fingers): Dark green long pod like vegetable, with a fury skin. They contain a lot of small seeds and are slimy in texture. They are used mainly in soups and stews, and are often included in salt fish and vegetable dishes.

PATTY: A very popular savoury pastry snack. The patty is a crescent shaped flaky pastry containing meat, fish or vegetables. They are usually quite hot and spicy.

PAPAYA (Pawpaw): A pear shaped fruit with yellow or orange skin when ripe. They have a pink or golden flesh inside filled with shiny black seeds, which are usually scooped out and discarded. The seeds are sometimes dried and used in seasoning. Papaya when unripe are used in soups, stews and vegetable dishes. Meat is wrapped in the leaves to tenderise it. Papaya are very nutritious and a good source of vitamin C.

PEAS: The term peas is usually used to refer to both peas and beans. The red kidney bean is used in the traditional rice and peas. Black eyed peas are white with a black eye, used fresh or dried. Gungo peas also known as pigeon peas are used fresh and dried. Available also in tins.

PEPPER, HOT : Hot peppers are a must in Jamaican cooking. Scotch bonnet is the hottest and most used pepper. However, others such as chillies and small 'bird peppers' are used. Peppers add a distinctive and splendid flavour to Jamaican cooking. They are added whole to soups, then removed before serving. A hot pepper sauce also known as pickappeppa is put on food or as a seasoning. Peppers are pickled with other vegetables to make a very hot accompaniment with meals. Jamaicans are not fainthearted when it comes to hot pepper.

PEPPER POT SOUP: popular traditional soup, which is hot and spicy originating from Africa. The main ingredient is callaloo.

PIMENTO: A tree producing allspice or Jamaican pepper. The flavour is a blend of cinnamon, cloves, mace and nutmeg. The berries are dried. Pimento berries are added to soup, stews meat and fish dishes. They are used in seasonings, marinades and drinks such as pimento liqueur. Traditional jerk cooking in Jamaica involved cooking a spicy barbecue dish in a fire pit on pimento wood.

PLANTAIN: A member of the banana family, the plantain looks like a very large banana.
Unlike the banana, the plantain cannot be eaten raw. When green or under ripe it is used as a boiled vegetable or made into chips. The ripe plantain is sliced and fried as a vegetable served with fried dumplings, saltfish and ackee. Very ripe ones can be used in sweet dishes such as plantain tarts.

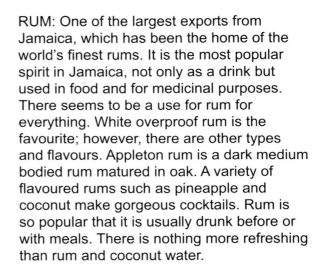

RICE & PEAS: One of the trademarks of Jamaican cooking. It consists usually of rice and red kidney beans. However, sometimes black eyed peas or gungo peas are used. It is usually served with meat dishes such as chicken and curry goat. It is also good with fish and some vegetable dishes.

RUM: One of the largest exports from Jamaica, which has been the home of the world's finest rums. It is the most popular spirit in Jamaica, not only as a drink but used in food and for medicinal purposes. There seems to be a use for rum for everything. White overproof rum is the favourite; however, there are other types and flavours. Appleton rum is a dark medium bodied rum matured in oak. A variety of flavoured rums such as pineapple and coconut make gorgeous cocktails. Rum is so popular that it is usually drunk before or with meals. There is nothing more refreshing than rum and coconut water.

RUNDOWN: A dish made mainly with salted mackerel in a seasoned coconut milk. It is usually served with boiled green bananas or white rice.

SALTFISH: This is dried salted cod. However, other fish is sometimes used. Salt fish is one half of Jamaica's national dish of ackee and saltfish.

SCOTCH BONNET PEPPER: A very hot pepper used in a lot of Jamaican cooking. It is used in soups, meat and fish dishes. As well as in pickles and seasoning.

SORREL: The red flower petals of a shrub are used to make a drink, which is a must at Christmas time in Jamaica. They are dried and stored for use.

SOURSOP: A fairly large fruit with a prickly green skin. Inside is a white succulent pulp with a sweet and sour delicate flavour. It has black shiny inedible seeds. Soursop is used for ice creams and drinks.

SWEET POTATO: A root vegetable which is similar to ordinary potato, but is sweet in flavour. They usually have red, pink, yellow, orange or white skins. The flesh is white, orange or yellow. The paler flesh varieties are drier in texture, whilst those with darker coloured flesh have more moisture. They are boiled, baked or fried. It is the essential ingredient for Jamaica's delicious potato pudding.

TAMARINDS: Long seed pods grown on a large tree. The pods have a brittle shell which contains a brown acid pulp with a toffee like consistency, surrounding large black seeds. The pulp can be eaten raw, added to savoury dishes such as curries, or made into a drink with water and sugar. Because of the sharp taste, tamarinds make good marinades and sauces. Tamarind balls are a favourite sweet for both adults and children.

TIE-A-LEAF (Blue drawers, Duckanoo): A pudding originating from Africa, traditionally tied and steamed in banana leaves. The main ingredients are cornmeal and coconut.

YAM: A starchy root vegetable, widely used in Jamaican cooking. The yam, which grows below a vine, comes in a variety of shapes and sizes. They have white or yellow flesh with a texture like potato. The white yam, which is softer, is more commonly used and will keep longer than the yellow. The yellow yam has a firmer texture when cooked. Yam is usually boiled and served as a vegetable or added to soups and stews. It can be boiled, baked, fried and mashed like potato.

INDEX